BEST

RAIN SHADOW HIKES

Western Washington

BEST

RAIN SHADOW HIKES

Western Washington

Michael Fagin and Skip Card

THE MOUNTAINEERS BOOKS

Michael Fagin dedicates this book to his wife, Elizabeth, for all her support and encouragement, and to his kids, Melissa and Brian, for keeping him company on some of his journeys into the rain shadow.

Skip Card dedicates this book to his parents, Bud and Donna Card, who took their son camping.

———————

Published by
The Mountaineers Books
1001 SW Klickitat Way, Suite 201
Seattle, WA 98134

Published simultaneously in Great Britain by Cordee, 3a DeMontfort Street, Leicester, England, LE1 7HD

Manufactured in Canada

"Green Trails" is a trademark of Green Trails, Inc., P.O. Box 77734, Seattle, WA 98177, (206) 762-MAPS.

Acquiring Editor: Margaret Sullivan
Project Editor: Christine Ummel Hosler
Copyeditor: Heath Lynn Silberfeld
Cover and book design: The Mountaineers Books
Layout: Mayumi Thompson
Cartographer: Moore Creative Design

Cover photograph: *Sheep Lake is the first lake you encounter hiking north on the Pacific Crest Trail north of Chinook Pass.* (Photo by Alan L. Bauer)
Frontispiece: *Field of asters along the Noble Knob Trail leading toward Mount Rainier* (Photo by Alan L. Bauer)

Library of Congress Cataloging-in-Publication Data
Fagin, Michael, 1950-
  Best rain shadow hikes in western Washington / Michael Fagin and Skip Card.— 1st ed.
    p.   cm.
  Includes bibliographical references (p.) and index.
  ISBN 0-89886-863-7
  1. Hiking—Washington (State), Western—Guidebooks. 2. Washington (State), Western—Guidebooks. I. Card, Skip, 1963- II. Title.
  GV199.42.W2 F34 2002
  796.52'2'09797—dc21   2002151427

CONTENTS

Introduction ■ 8

OLYMPICS RAIN SHADOW ■ 35
1. Mount Constitution ■ 37
2. Fidalgo Head Loop ■ 40
3. Dungeness Spit ■ 43
4. Deer Park to Obstruction Point ■ 46
5. Mount Townsend ■ 49
6. Buckhorn Mountain ■ 52
7. Mount Ellinor ■ 55
8. Ebey's Landing ■ 57

NORTH CASCADES EAST RAIN SHADOW ■ 61
9. Canyon Creek ■ 63
10. Gold Ridge Tarn ■ 66
11. Ferguson Lake ■ 69
12. Pugh Ridge ■ 72

STEVENS PASS EAST RAIN SHADOW ■ 75
13. Basalt Pass ■ 77
14. Alpine Lookout ■ 80
15. Lake Julius, Loch Eileen, and Lake Donald ■ 84
16. Larch Lake ■ 87
17. Windy Pass ■ 90
18. Colchuck Lake ■ 93
19. Jack Creek to Meadow Creek ■ 96

SALMON LA SAC RAIN SHADOW ■ 99
20. Polallie Ridge to Diamond Lake ■ 101
21. Kachess Ridge to West Peak ■ 103
22. Peggy's Pond ■ 106
23. Davis Peak ■ 109

TEANAWAY RAIN SHADOW ■ 113
24. Lake Ann ■ 115
25. Lake Ingalls ■ 118
26. Bean Creek Basin ■ 122
27. Iron Peak ■ 124
28. Ingalls Creek ■ 127
29. Miller Peak ■ 131
30. Iron Creek to Teanaway Ridge ■ 133

31. Tronsen Ridge ■ 135
32. Navaho Pass ■ 139
33. North Fork Taneum Creek/Taneum Ridge ■ 142

MOUNT RAINIER RAIN SHADOW ■ 147
34. Kelly Butte ■ 149
35. Grand Park ■ 151
36. Burroughs Mountain ■ 154
37. Hidden Lake ■ 157
38. Slide Mountain ■ 159
39. Noble Knob ■ 162
40. Norse Peak ■ 165
41. Crystal Peak ■ 167

SOUTH CASCADES RAIN SHADOW ■ 171
42. Sourdough Gap ■ 173
43. Fifes Ridge ■ 175
44. Mount Aix ■ 178
45. Goat Peak/American Ridge ■ 181
46. Tumac Mountain ■ 184
47. Blankenship Lakes ■ 187
48. Indian Creek ■ 190
49. Killen Creek ■ 193
50. Indian Heaven ■ 196

References ■ 201
Suggested Reading ■ 202
Index ■ 203
Acknowledgments ■ 205

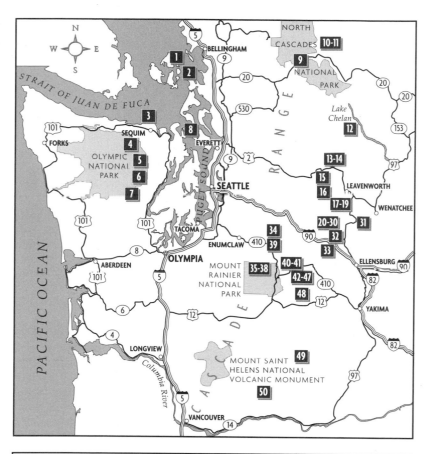

INTRODUCTION

If you can see Mount Rainier, it's going to rain. If you can't see Mount Rainier, it's raining already.
—Early Western Washington weather forecast

The Pacific Northwest has a soggy reputation. It started (at least by European standards) when the Lewis and Clark expedition camped along the territorial coastline one wet winter and filled damp journals with entries such as "Rained all day, nothing to report." The reputation grew as pioneers and settlers mailed ink-smeared letters back East that dripped with laments about mud, moss, and gray skies. It continues today as local forecasters cram phrases like "showers turning to rain," "rain mixed with showers," and "intermittent showers followed by periods of rain" into a typical three-day forecast. Only in Washington do locals feel a sense of meteorological optimism when the outlook shifts from "partly cloudy" to "partly sunny."

But the Evergreen State also has its bright spots, sheltered places where an almost magical blend of geography and meteorology seems to raise an invisible umbrella over a valley or mountainside. Certain parts of Washington can receive heavy rain during a particular storm while nearby areas see little or no precipitation. Mount Olympus averages roughly 200 inches of precipitation each year on its snowcapped slopes, but the town of Sequim just 35 miles away typically gets only 16.7 inches. Snoqualmie Pass averages 104.7 inches of rain each year, yet nearby Blewett Pass between Cle Elum and Leavenworth gets just 34.7 inches.

Meteorologists say these large contrasts in local rainfall are the result of Washington's rare combination of ocean, mountains, and prevailing west winds. That's the short explanation. To really understand how geography, topography, and atmosphere can make one county damp while leaving its neighbor dry requires a short course on weather basics.

Entire textbooks are dedicated to meteorology, and several are listed at the end of this book. The following pages offer a basic exploration of the local weather principles that led to the selection of fifty scenic trails where hikers are more likely to see sun than get soaked. This section also includes some basics of mountain meteorology and some tools readers can use to forecast weather during summer hikes.

WEATHER BASICS I:
CONTINENTAL CLIMATE AND MARINE CLIMATE

Washington state has a split weather personality. Prevailing winds and proximity to the ocean are two factors that create the two vastly different types of climates found in the state's eastern and western halves. Western

Slate Peak is crowned with a lovely fire lookout. (Photo by Alan L. Bauer)

Washington has a marine climate, while Eastern Washington has a continental climate.

Winds are one reason behind this regional difference. In the mid-latitudes—the area ranging from 30 degrees to 60 degrees north of the equator—winds generally blow from the west. Winds are named for the direction from which they originate, so winds blowing west to east are called "westerly" winds.

Hikers on the summit of Mount Ellinor look through the clouds at Mount Washington. (Photo by Skip Card)

Westerly winds reach Washington state after traveling across the Pacific Ocean, which has very limited seasonal temperature variation compared to the North American interior. The average surface temperature of the waters in the northeast Pacific Ocean due west of Washington state is 48 degrees F in winter and 60 degrees F in summer—a relatively minor difference in a year of seasonal fluctuations when compared to extremes in continental locations. The ocean's moderating influence means a city like Seattle will experience relatively minor seasonal variations between temperature highs and lows compared to cities in the continent's interior that are far away from the moderating influence of ocean air. Seattle's summertime temperatures tend to be cooler and its winter temperatures tend to be warmer than the extremes found in cities where the weather is affected largely by winds that sweep over land. The more subtle seasonal differences in climate close to the ocean can be seen in the table below as one compares Seattle to more inland cities such as Spokane and Bismarck, North Dakota, both of which reflect a typical continental climate.

CITY	JANUARY temperatures (high/low)	JULY temperatures (high/low)	JANUARY rainfall (inches)	JULY rainfall (inches)
Seattle	45°F/35°F	75°F/55°F	5.70	0.78
Spokane	33°F/22°F	84°F/56°F	1.99	0.56
Bismarck	21°F/0°F	84°F/56°F	0.45	2.58

WEATHER BASICS 2: MOUNTAIN RANGES AND CLOUDS

The moist Pacific air does not breeze into Washington state unimpeded. It abruptly slams into the Olympic Mountains and the Cascades. In many ways, the presence of these prominent mountains creates the most important variable in local weather patterns.

Air in mountain areas is rarely at rest. Air moving west to east is forced to rise when it reaches the western slopes of the Cascades and Olympics. Once past the crest, the air is forced downward on the mountains' eastern slopes. (See Figure 1.)

Air cools as it rises and warms as it sinks. Specifically, air cools 5.5 degrees F for every 1000 feet that it rises, and it gains 5.5 degrees for every 1000 feet it falls. This temperature change is called the *adiabatic lapse rate*. It is not a fixed rate of change. The lapse rate is less if the air is saturated, which is generally the case around Puget Sound for air going up. The important thing is that the state's mountains dramatically change the westerly winds' air temperature at the same time that they impede the winds' eastward progress.

The temperature of an air mass determines more than whether you will need to slip on a sweater during a hike. Temperature also affects how much water vapor the air contains before clouds form and, potentially, rain falls. Compared to cool air, warm air can contain much more water vapor before the air becomes saturated. The concentration of water vapor in saturated air at 72 degrees F is double that of air at 50 degrees. And you do not have to go to the mountains to test this principle. Just put some ice in a drink and watch the sides of the glass become wet with beads of condensation. The cold glass hasn't magically attracted the moisture in the air. The air around the glass has merely cooled to a point where it has become saturated and condensation has formed.

The combination of ocean, mountains, and prevailing westerly winds creates conditions that often leave Washington's western slopes drenched with rain while its eastern slopes stay relatively dry. The process is rather predictable. Air moves west across the ocean into Washington and is forced to rise when it hits the state's mountains. As it rises, the air cools. This

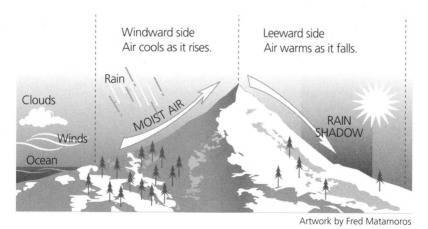

Artwork by Fred Matamoros

Figure 1. Mountains affect Washington's meteorology.

cooler air becomes saturated, so clouds form. Clouds lead to rain, which falls on the mountains' western slopes. Once the air passes over the crest of the mountains, it loses elevation and the air warms as it descends the eastern slopes. This warm air becomes "sub-saturated," so the clouds dissipate and the rain stops—at least until the air hits the next big mountain range.

WEATHER BASICS 3: THE RAIN SHADOW EFFECT

Westerly winds, Washington's mountain ranges, rising air on the west slopes, and sinking air on the east slopes create areas that meteorologists call a "rain shadow." The term can be confusing, since "rain shadow" can make you think "rain forest"—only darker. However, rain shadow areas are places where people are likely to find less rain and more sunshine. Virtually all of the state's rain shadow areas lie on the east slopes of the Cascades and, to a lesser extent, the east slopes of the Olympics. The rain shadow areas can be seen on a map showing Washington state precipitation patterns (see Figure 2).

The rain shadow effect can create very different rainfall totals in areas that are close to one another. For example, Stevens Pass gets 81.54 inches of rainfall a year, while the town of Leavenworth, only 27 miles due east, gets 25.32 inches a year.

Average Annual Precipitation
Amounts shown in inches

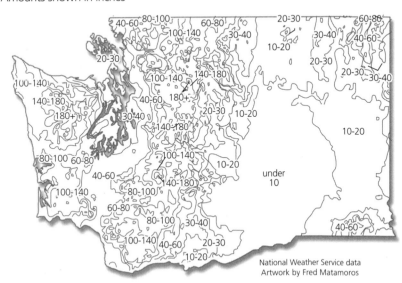

National Weather Service data
Artwork by Fred Matamoros

Figure 2. Washington's heaviest rainfall occurs on the Pacific Coast and near the crest of its mountain ranges.

WEATHER BASICS 4: LOW PRESSURE AND HIGH PRESSURE

Forecasting Washington's weather would be simpler if all weather forecasters had to consider was prevailing westerly winds and a few mountain ranges. But Northwest weather patterns are rarely so constant and predictable. Seattle and other Puget Sound cities receive far more precipitation in winter than in summer. The major reason for this variation in rainfall is that the storm track across the Pacific in winter is usually far enough south to bring Washington state a more or less regular series of weather disturbances. In summer, this storm activity is less severe and usually farther north. These changes are tied to seasonal differences in the strengths and locations of two semi-permanent pressure centers: the Aleutian Low and the Pacific High.

The vast differences caused in the region by these seasonal cycles is particularly apparent in local rainfall totals. Between November and March, Western Washington typically gets heavy rain in the lowlands and snow in the mountains, while the inland areas of Eastern Washington often see light snowfall, colder temperatures, and consecutive days of fog. The town of Forks just off Washington's coast typically gets 77 inches of rain from October through March, an average of about 13 inches per month. But the same town is much drier in the summer months of June, July, and August, when the same location averages just 2.73 inches of rain per month.

Changes in atmospheric pressure are often excellent indicators of upcoming weather. We may not consciously feel the weight of all the air molecules piled atop our heads, but they are there, pressing down on us. At sea level, the weight of all the air pressing against the Earth—a calculation known as barometric pressure—averages 1013 millibars, or 29.92 inches of mercury. Pressure decreases with increasing elevation. The summit of 14,410-foot Mount Rainier typically has 40 percent less air pressure than cities at sea level.

In a low-pressure system, the air tends to rise. Rising air cools, and cooling air tends to form clouds. Conversely, in high-pressure systems the air tends to sink, and as air sinks it warms. Warm air holds moisture better, so clouds tend to dissipate.

The Aleutian Low and the Pacific High tend to dominate Western Washington weather each winter and summer, respectively. Storms associated with the Aleutian Low that sweep in off the Pacific will usually start affecting Washington's weather patterns in October and last until sometime in April. Around May, the Pacific High strengthens and moves north, eventually creating summer weather that is typically dry and clear with light winds.

These patterns repeat every year but they do not always arrive on schedule. Sometimes the Pacific storms do not begin affecting the region until November, leading to excellent hiking conditions well into the fall. However, they also can arrive early, spoiling the outdoor party as early as mid-September.

The seasonal cycles in the weather in this region, as elsewhere, are prone to interruptions. At times, Washington state is dominated by what meteorologists call a *blocking high,* a mass of high pressure in the upper atmosphere stretching to more than 20,000 feet. This pattern is often in place by mid-July, and the driest period in the Seattle area is typically between July 27 and August 3. Blocking highs also can arrive during winter, and such a system can last for a week or more. The high's arrival can mean sunny skies for skiers and snowshoers, but a high that lingers in winter often causes a serious interruption in the weather systems that replenish the winter snowpack, the source of most of the state's water supply. Most droughts can be attributed to blocking highs that arrived in winter and stayed too long.

WEATHER BASICS 5: WARM FRONTS AND COLD FRONTS

The precipitation associated with low-pressure systems is often concentrated in bands along *warm fronts* and *cold fronts.* In a warm front, the air moving into the region is warmer than the air that it is replacing. When a warm front arrives, the warm air typically slides up and over cooler, denser air. The warm air cools as it rises, and clouds form once the air becomes saturated.

When a warm front sweeps into the Northwest, high clouds are usually followed by lower clouds and eventually light precipitation. Warm fronts that blow through Seattle during fall and winter often create a day or two of steady drizzle or light rain and poor visibility.

Cold fronts affect areas differently. When cold fronts move through Western Washington, usually a strong westerly flow forces the moist air from the ocean to rise up and over the west slopes of the Olympics and Cascades. This causes clouds and precipitation that often linger for days

Yet Western Washington's cold fronts are special. Since the cold front travels a great distance over the ocean before arriving in the state, this cold air tends to warm significantly. A cold air mass coming from Alaska can be 10 to 20 degrees F, but it has many hundreds of miles to travel across the Pacific Ocean to reach Seattle. With the Pacific Ocean at about 52 degrees F, the air above the ocean will warm this cold air mass as it travels south. By the time the air mass reaches Seattle, it has warmed significantly. Regions that lack an ocean's moderating influence see much more dynamic weather when cold fronts arrive. Eastern Washington tends to see clear skies once a cold front has moved through, since with this westerly flow the air is forced down the east slope of the Cascades. In the Midwest, cold fronts often bring significant temperature extremes, heavy rain, and thunderstorms.

WEATHER BASICS 6: THE JET STREAM

Closely linked to Washington's low-pressure systems and its warm and cold fronts is what meteorologists call the *jet stream,* a shifting river of westerly wind about 30,000 feet above sea level within which the air can reach

Facing page: During low moisture years, the upper reaches of Indian Creek dry up. (Photo by Alan L. Bauer)

speeds of up to 200 miles per hour. The jet stream helps mix up the atmosphere, transporting cold air out of the north and bringing warm air up from the south. Storms tend to form along the jet stream, so cities in the stream's path generally see wet weather in winter. But the jet stream does not stay in one place long. In winter, its main current meanders between 30 degrees and 60 degrees latitude, a region stretching roughly from Los Angeles, California, to Juneau, Alaska. (Washington state lies mostly between 46 degrees and 49 degrees latitude, right in the middle of the jet stream's home turf.) During a typical wet winter, the jet stream will often be pointed at Washington, bringing storms in rapid succession to the state.

WEATHER BASICS 7: LA NIÑA AND EL NIÑO

All the weather phenomena presented to this point are likely familiar to any longtime Northwest resident—or at least resonate with people who regularly watch the weather forecast on the local news. It is here, it is local. Winters are wet, summers are nice. Fronts and pressure zones blow in from the Pacific Ocean, conditions change a lot.

But Northwest weather patterns also can be affected by changes in sea surface temperatures in ocean areas close to the equator. One weather cycle that creates the biggest impact is the El Niño Southern Oscillation, known as ENSO to meteorologists and "El Niño" to everyone else. The effects of El Niño are felt more in winter, and rarely in summer, but the impact they can have on winter snowfall often determines how soon hiking trails become snow-free.

During an El Niño or warm ENSO event in the eastern tropical Pacific Ocean, the trade winds blowing from the east are weaker than normal and the sea surface temperature is warmer than normal. This change disrupts worldwide atmospheric circulation. During a strong El Niño, storms hitting the West Coast of the United States have a greater tendency to hit California. Washington state typically ends up with above-average temperatures and below-average rainfall in the winter. Mountain areas often see less snow and higher freezing levels. Winter skiing conditions can be bad and summer water shortages can occur, but trails often melt out in late spring rather than early summer.

In other years, sea surface temperatures are well below average in the eastern tropical Pacific. This opposite situation, known as a "La Niña" event, often creates winter conditions in Washington that lead to below-average temperatures and above-average mountain snowfall. During the La Niña winter of 1998–99, so many storms swept into the region that the weather gauge at Mount Baker Ski Area recorded 304 inches of snow in February alone. Mount Baker ultimately recorded 1140 inches of snow over twelve months, a figure later accepted by the National Climate Data Center as a world record for annual snowfall. The old record had been recorded at the Paradise Ranger Station on Mount Rainier, where 1122 inches of snow fell in 1971–72.

WEATHER BASICS 8: PUGET SOUND CONVERGENCE ZONE

What forecasters call the "Puget Sound Convergence Zone" takes many of Washington's basic weather effects and channels them together to produce some nasty conditions in the western Cascades and over Puget Sound. Some people call the Puget Sound Convergence Zone the "Twilight Zone" of weather.

After a cold front passes, a strong west to northwest wind sets up. The Olympic Mountains impede these winds, splitting much of the incoming air in two directions. Part of the incoming air is channeled through the Strait of Juan de Fuca, and another branch flows south of the Olympics through the Chehalis Gap. Then the two wind masses converge, usually north of Seattle near Everett. (See Figure 3.)

When these winds converge, the moist ocean air is forced to rise. Rising air cools, so clouds form and rain falls. The precipitation is concentrated in

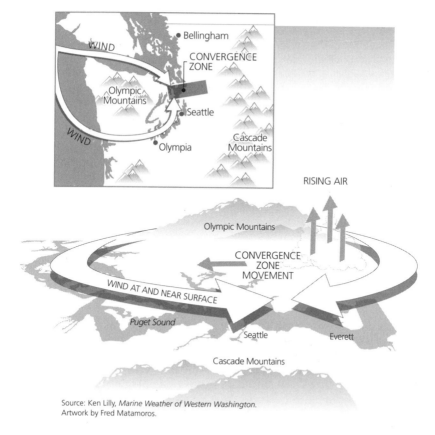

Source: Ken Lilly, *Marine Weather of Western Washington.*
Artwork by Fred Matamoros.

Figure 3. The Puget Sound Convergence Zone

an east–west band extending from Puget Sound to the Cascades. The exact location and evolution of the convergence zone's rainfall depend on hard-to-predict details in the air flow coming from the Pacific. Rainfall typically moves south and often (but by no means always) dissipates before reaching Sea-Tac Airport.

In the mountains, the Convergence Zone favors an area from Stevens Pass south toward Snoqualmie Pass. This mountainous area can receive copious amounts of precipitation when the zone effect is under way, and 20 inches of snow falling in 24 hours is not uncommon.

Winds can converge in the zone any time of the year, but the effect is most common during spring. And it is deceiving. When the zone is active, Seattle sometimes falls under a rain shadow caused by the Olympic Mountains. While Everett is getting drenched, hiking and biking in Seattle parks can often be sunny and pleasant experiences. At other times, the Convergence Zone can produce extreme weather that causes thunderstorms and, on rare occasions, small tornadoes.

WEATHER BASICS 9: MARINE PUSH

Another headache for Washington weather forecasters occurs when barometric pressure on the coast is higher than in areas close to Puget Sound. Since winds tend to travel from high-pressure zones to low-pressure zones, this pressure difference forces moist marine air inland, an effect known as the *marine push.*

During spring and summer, the marine push can be weak and its primary effect is to spread low clouds throughout Western Washington. Such clouds usually dissipate by noon. If the marine push is stronger, light drizzle or moderate precipitation can occur throughout Western Washington, although Eastern Washington will usually remain dry.

A weak marine push generally occurs when the barometric pressure in Hoquiam on the Washington coast is about two millibars higher than the pressure in Seattle. This will usually bring winds traveling at 10 miles per hour from the southwest, moving air inland from the coast. With this wind will come low clouds, often hovering at about 2000 feet but sometimes rising to 5000 or 6000 feet. These pushes usually are dry patterns, but they can produce drizzle in some areas. Rain shadow regions typically stay dry or partly cloudy during weak marine pushes.

The strong marine push is a different animal. The most common strong marine push occurs when Puget Sound has two to three days of warm weather with highs topping 85 degrees. This usually causes low pressure to form over Puget Sound, creating a pressure difference between the Sound and the coast. If the pressure difference is significant enough—if, for example, pressure at Hoquiam exceeds pressure in Seattle by 6 millibars or more—it can generate winds from the southwest in excess of 20 miles per hour. These strong winds bring clouds from the coast that produce some major cooling. Under the influence of a strong marine push, Seattle can see

90 degrees and sunshine one day and 60 degrees with rain the next. Mountain areas in the Olympics and western Cascades will have light to moderate precipitation and poor visibility during a strong marine push. The east slopes of the Cascades may get lucky and stay dry or partly cloudy.

WEATHERS BASICS 10: LIGHTNING

Despite the rain shadow effect, many regions east of the Cascades crest are prone to summer thunderstorms. Lightning can strike at any time, but storms generally occur after noon. (Hikers who wrap up their treks early in the day decrease their odds of getting struck. Such hikers also stay cooler, since exposed trails on south-facing slopes can have 115-degree F heat radiating from the rocks.)

In Washington, thunderstorms generally occur when hot weather and an associated trough of low pressure near the surface combine to create unstable conditions. But another source of summer storms is what meteorologists call the *summer monsoonal flow*. Although typically associated with heavy rains, the term *monsoon* refers simply to wind that arises from the temperature difference between a land mass and an adjacent ocean. Wind shifts direction as temperatures change with the seasons.

The most famous monsoons are found in southern Asia and affect the Himalayas, the lofty mountain range that includes Mount Everest. In winter and early spring, cold air forms a zone of high pressure over the Himalayas, causing wind to descend from the mountains toward areas of relatively low pressure over the Indian Ocean. Climbers often take advantage of a late spring weather window to make their summit attempts. However, by late May or early June the pressure zones have become reversed, and soon moisture-laden air begins to blow in from the warm Indian Ocean, bringing huge volumes of rain to the mountains' slopes.

The U.S. Southwest has its own monsoonal flows. The

Figure 4. The fair weather altocumulus cloud buildup occurs often in the hot eastern zones of our area.
(Photo by Alan L. Bauer)

Figure 5. Moderate altocumulus cloud vertical development is the second stage of a developing thunderstorm cloud, as seen over Eastern Washington. (Photo by Alan L. Bauer)

Mexican Monsoon or Arizona Monsoon occurs in summer when winds blow from the south and bring moisture from the Gulf of California and the interior of Mexico. The moisture fuels thunderstorms in Arizona, but moist air also gets carried into the upper atmosphere and transported north. Most of the moisture falls in southern Utah and Colorado, but at times it drifts into Oregon and even southern Washington. When it arrives, thunderstorms often follow.

Hikers who sense an approaching thunderstorm should quickly head for lower ground. Weather experts say they can often tell a thunderstorm is approaching because they feel the hairs on their head, neck, or arms standing up. However, cumulus clouds are a better indicator.

Look at the clouds' shapes. If the clouds are wider than they are tall, this implies stable conditions and indicates little chance of a storm in the short term. This is the case with fair-weather altocumulus clouds

Figure 6. Towering cumulus thunderstorms build in the summer over the Cascades. (Photo by Alan L. Bauer)

(Figure 4). If the cloud is showing more vertical development (Figure 5), lightning might soon develop, particularly if storms are in the forecast. Climbers and hikers should use caution to make sure they do not get caught on an exposed slope during a lightning storm—especially if they carry metal walking sticks, climbing hardware, or a metal-frame backpack.

If a cumulonimbus cloud (Figure 6) forms, lightning is likely imminent. Anyone in the open should quickly descend to safety.

DIVINE FORECASTING

A meteorologist who stands gazing at the heavens might be seeking divine help in the next prediction or asking forgiveness for messing up another forecast. But most forecasters who scan the skies are practicing the ancient art of cloud watching, a critical forecasting skill that can help anyone who doesn't have access to the latest radar scans and satellite images.

Clouds change character in a distinct progression as a warm front approaches Washington state, and each change of mood can provide an indication of incoming weather. To illustrate this idea, imagine yourself in a typical morning scenario.

You awake at 6:00 A.M. on a Friday in Seattle and eagerly get the coffee ready in preparation for taking the kids on their first camping trip. The goal is to hike a short distance somewhere near Snoqualmie Pass, find a tent site, roast some marshmallows, and, above all, stay dry.

Gazing to the west, you see some beautiful, wispy cirrus clouds moving in (Figure 7). These thin, fibrous clouds hover above 16,500 feet and consist of ice crystals. Sometimes they act as miniature prisms and split sunlight into its component colors, creating a halo effect. Clouds such as these do not produce precipitation, so you decide there is little to worry about for now.

As you gather the camping gear, you pick up your altimeter and take a reading. The altimeter puts you at 300 feet above sea level. Most altimeters rely on changes in barometric pressure to calculate elevation, so the devices also can be used to forecast weather. Hikers who remain at a fixed

Figure 7. Cirrus clouds on a fair day in the Snoqualmie Valley. (Photo by Alan L. Bauer)

Figure 8. Cirrus clouds with mare's tails float high above the Snoqualmie Valley. (Photo by Alan L. Bauer)

position but see their altitude rising can tell that the surrounding air pressure is dropping, an indication of a low-pressure system and the possible arrival of a wet warm front. (The rule of thumb is to monitor the altimeter every 3 hours and look for a trend. If altitude rises 80 feet every 3 hours, a wet low-pressure system is probably on the way.)

By the time you finish breakfast, it is 9:00 A.M., and your altimeter now reads 370 feet—a sign that the air pressure is dropping. Looking west, you see more cirrus clouds that almost cover the entire sky (Figure 8). The clouds with the hooks are nicknamed "mare's tails" and usually indicate strong winds in the jet stream. All signs are beginning to indicate an impending weather disturbance.

Soon you see a jet plane that has left in its path a lingering trail of condensation that stretches across the sky (Figure 9). This marks a change from the previous day, when jets' contrails were small and quickly faded. Large, lingering contrails mean more moisture is in the air, another sign that a warm front is advancing.

You begin to reconsider your camping plans. Turning on the radio, you hear the forecaster predict a 50 percent chance of rain on the coast. The pace of your packing slows. Taking another look at the sky, you see a beautiful halo ringing the sun (Figure 10).

The kids awake at 10:00 A.M., and the first thing they notice is that you do not have any marshmallows. On your way to the grocery store, you catch a glimpse of Mount Rainier and see a large, mushroom-shaped cloud cap covering the summit (Figure 11). Seeing this type of cloud, known as a "lenticular," changes your plans.

A lenticular cloud atop a mountain peak indicates strong winds in the upper atmosphere and high-level moisture, two ingredients that often signal the arrival of a warm front. The combination of falling barometric pressure and a lenticular cloud that follows the previous cloud patterns will bring rain to the region 90 percent of the time.

Figure 9. Condensation trails of numerous jets cover the western sky above a coulee wall in the Columbia National Wildlife Refuge. (Photo by Alan L. Bauer)

Figure 10. The sun being ringed by a halo is a sign of an incoming front. (Photo by Alan L. Bauer)

Lenticular clouds can occur atop all major volcanoes in the state, as well as nonvolcanic mountains such as Mount Stuart. The clouds can sometimes be stacked vertically, several atop each other. At other times, winds can blow them away from a mountain peak and spread a dozen or more across the nearby sky. Lenticulars are known as "orographic" or "mountain-induced" clouds.

By the time you return with the marshmallows, the cloud deck is falling, and so are your hopes of happy camping. You cancel the trip—at least for now.

Figure 11. A lenticular cloud seen northeast of Mount Rainier. A sighting of this type of cloud is usually followed by rain or snow within twenty-four hours. (Photo by Frank Sincock)

Later, you spot a sheetlike altostratus cloud (Figure 12) hovering in the same middle-level (or "alto") elevation as the lenticular. This altostratus cloud is made up of water droplets, unlike the wispy cirrus clouds that consisted of ice crystals. Altostratus clouds sometimes produce a brief shower, but that is about all.

By Friday afternoon, the radio is reporting rain on the coast. Above your house now hover lower stratus clouds (Figure 13). Your altimeter keeps rising, indicating falling air pressure. Everything signals wet weather is on the way.

By dinnertime, you see thick nimbostratus clouds (Figure 14) and rain is falling in Seattle. An outing to Snoqualmie Pass is out, so you decide instead to head on Saturday for the rain shadow area in the Teanaway region east of Snoqualmie Pass. After a warm front and cold front pass, this area will likely be dry.

Saturday, you drive through a heavy downpour in North Bend, probably the result of the Puget Sound Convergence Zone. Skies are still gray as you cross Snoqualmie Pass, and the passengers in your vehicle are wondering aloud if they will be forced to camp in the rain.

Then, a strange thing happens. You head toward Cle Elum, and the sun is shining. As you exit toward the Teanaway River, you feel dry air carried by westerly winds. The skeptics in your vehicle praise your forecasting skills.

And it all feels just divine.

Figure 12. Altostratus clouds, marking an incoming warm front, cover the sky in the Quilomene Wildlife Area of central Washington. (Photo by Alan L. Bauer)

Figure 13. Stratus clouds fully cover the sky hours before the rain begins from an approaching front. (Photo by Alan Bauer)

Figure 14. Nimbostratus clouds smoothly cover the sky during a hard winter storm along the Middle Fork Snoqualmie River. (Photo by Alan Bauer)

HIKING SAFELY IN RAIN SHADOW AREAS

In selecting the fifty rain shadow hikes in this book, we have done extensive research to discover which scenic areas of Western Washington receive the least rainfall. We also have tromped the trails, driven to the trailheads, pored over maps, and double-checked facts and figures to make sure the directions, elevations, and mileages are as accurate as possible. Armed with this book, hikers should be able to head confidently into the wilderness while feeling optimistic that their chosen trails have a good chance of leading them toward sunny skies rather than a drenching downpour.

Having said that, we offer this caution: Northwest weather is notoriously unpredictable, forecasts are sometimes incorrect, and even rain shadow areas get rained on sometimes. Hiking in a rain shadow increases the odds of finding sunshine and dry trails, but the tips and trails suggested here cannot guarantee a pleasant experience, or even a rain-free one. Hikers should always travel equipped to cope with severe weather and be prepared to handle most common emergencies.

The best advice for summer trips in the Pacific Northwest is to travel prepared for bad weather. Hikers planning to cover any significant distance should always carry a windproof and rain-repellent jacket or poncho so they can stay dry during a downpour.

The jacket, however, is just one piece of a hiker's necessary equipment. For generations, the wilderness courses taught by The Mountaineers and other outdoor groups have stressed bringing a backpack stuffed with "The Ten Essentials" listed here:

1. *Extra clothing,* to provide warmth and dryness.
2. *Extra food,* enough in case you are forced to spend a night in the woods.
3. *Sunglasses,* especially when traveling on snow.
4. *Knife,* crucial for some first-aid procedures and for whittling wood into kindling.
5. *Firestarter,* either a candle or a resin-saturated commercial product designed to help you burn wet wood.
6. *First-aid kit,* stocked and ready to use.
7. *Matches,* stored in a watertight container.
8. *Flashlight,* preferably with extra batteries.
9. *Map* of the area where you will be hiking.
10. *Compass,* and the knowledge to use it.

Many longtime hikers do not stop with these ten items. For most, a crucial "eleventh essential" is a working knowledge of wilderness skills, such as how to read a map, plot your location, start a fire, or build a temporary shelter. Similarly, a first-aid kit stocked with a variety of fancy tourniquets or compresses is little use to someone who has not taken a basic course in handling common wilderness emergencies. Equipment is no substitute for skill.

New portable technologies, such as Global Positioning Satellite (GPS) units or wireless telephones, can help hikers chart a course or, if lost, call for assistance. Yet these devices should *not* be considered substitutes for any of the hiking essentials, nor should they be seen as mechanical licenses to take unacceptable risks. Countless backcountry travelers who have carried a wireless telephone into a Washington wilderness area have learned too late that the state's undulating topography creates many dead spots where wireless signals are neither sent nor received. Similarly, thick clouds or dense trees can prevent handheld GPS units from receiving the clear satellite signals necessary to pinpoint a location. Both devices are prone to mechanical breakdowns and dead batteries.

Outdoor groups such as The Mountaineers offer excellent courses in the basics of wilderness travel, as do many of the growing number of commercial guide services and outfitters that now operate throughout Washington state. Also available are a number of books designed to teach backcountry basics. One of the books most recommended is *Mountaineering: Freedom of the Hills,* a comprehensive volume of backcountry wisdom published and regularly updated by The Mountaineers Books.

HOW TO USE THIS GUIDEBOOK

Anyone familiar with trail guides in the *100 Hikes* series from The Mountaineers Books should quickly recognize the helpful patterns echoed in this book. If so, you know the drill. If not, it will be especially helpful for you to know some basics.

Trails are grouped throughout this book by rain shadow region and listed in roughly the order a hiker would encounter them while driving from trailhead to trailhead. Each trail description begins with a standard set of facts designed to give readers an at-a-glance summary of each trail's length and difficulty.

"Distance" refers to the mileage hikers should expect to cover if they trek the trails as described. In many cases, optional side trips are suggested that would increase the mileage. Of course, hikers are always free to halt their trips short of the goal if they feel tired, sense a storm approaching, or are running out of food or water.

"Hiking time" is a rough calculation of the number of hours a typical adult would need to cover the described route. It is based largely on the idea that a person of average fitness travels about 2 miles per hour on up-hill terrain and 3 miles per hour going downhill. Your own speed may vary, perhaps considerably. The posted time does not include any minutes (or hours) spent resting or taking in the views, so always add a little extra time when planning a trip.

"Starting elevation" is the best estimate of the trailhead altitude. These will likely differ from the elevations shown in green ink on the popular Green Trails maps, which round off trailhead heights to the nearest 100 feet, but it should closely match the map's tiny contour lines. In most cases, the starting elevations listed here are based on a combination of map research and GPS readings taken at the trailheads. "High point," calculated much the same way, gives hikers the best estimate of where each trail tops out.

"Hikable" refers to the months when each trail is typically free of snow to the extent that people can tromp the path without pausing too often to find the route in the melting snowpack. This is always an estimate, and it varies year to year depending on how much snow fell in winter and how long it lingered in spring. The information is also highly subjective, since what one hiker sees as a muddy rut or a slightly swollen stream might appear to another hiker to be an impassable barrier. For the most up-to-date route conditions, we urge hikers to call the contacts listed under "Information" and ask about the state of specific trails. Phone numbers can change frequently, but all were accurate when this book went to press.

"Maps" lists the specific maps that show the trail's exact route. In most cases, these are produced by Green Trails, Custom Correct, or the United States Geological Survey (USGS). Maps produced by the U.S. Forest Service are not listed but often are available at ranger stations for a modest charge. In most cases, Forest Service maps are the best available guides to the roads leading to the trailheads—important information on public lands where roads close, open, change names, or change course with startling frequency.

Significant efforts have been made to make sure the trail descriptions—and in particular the elevations, mileage estimates, and driving directions to the trailheads—are as accurate as possible. In most cases, information regarding elevations and trail distances is based on maps produced by

View of Upper Crystal Lake and distant Mount Rainier from just past Sourdough Gap along the Pacific Crest Trail. (Photo by Alan. L. Bauer)

Seattle-based Green Trails, Inc., the leading producer of trail maps in Washington state. Green Trails data were often double-checked against other maps. Previous guidebooks published by The Mountaineers Books—in particular those in the *100 Hikes* series by Ira Spring and Harvey Manning—also were used as references. Finally, whenever possible, we recorded GPS readings when on the trails to gauge elevation, and these readings often confirmed distances by a dead reckoning based on estimates of average hiking speeds.

Maps, Mileages, and Elevations

The maps produced for this book were created to give hikers a clear idea of hiking routes, distances, and elevation changes, but they are not meant to be substitutes for the detailed trail maps that all responsible wilderness visitors should carry. Elevation contours and trail distances shown in the maps produced for this book are based on Green Trails maps, with permission from Green Trails and its president, Alan Coburn.

Despite our attention to detail and accuracy, we offer the usual cautions: Few guidebooks are perfect, and none is ageless. Trails can change their paths over time. New trails sometimes appear, with new junctions. Crucial directional signs can be stolen or destroyed. Road names change. And even

Low stratus fog covers Fifes Ridge in the early morning.
(Photo by Alan L. Bauer)

the distance estimates and elevation contours of the best maps are simply cartographers' educated guesses. The authors and The Mountaineers Books urge all hikers to use the information published in this guidebook as a supplement to up-to-date trail maps, and to call or visit the U.S. Forest Service or other land managers to learn current conditions.

Trail Profiles

Trailhead elevations and high points give some idea of how much uphill effort will be required during a hike, but they do not tell the whole story. In the rolling terrain of the Northwest, trails regularly rise and fall as the paths ascend ridges, dip down to cross streams, or follow the rolling flow of undulating meadows.

The trail profiles that accompany the maps give a more complete picture of what is in store. But the profiles are not designed to reflect every tiny dip and spike in the paths. Use them to get a general idea of where the trails gain and lose elevation or change pitch.

Permits, Fees, and the Northwest Forest Pass

The days when a hiker could drive up to a trailhead anywhere in the woods, park for free, and walk into the wild without filling out a form are just about over. Today, the crush of people who want to explore Washington's scenic areas often force land managers to monitor recreational use and limit overnight stays in fragile areas. In addition, hikers are being asked increasingly to pay a greater share of the costs of trail maintenance.

When parking at many of the trailheads listed in this guidebook, hikers will be required to post a Northwest Forest Pass on their vehicles. This pass, part of the experimental Fee Demonstration Project authorized by Congress, costs $30 and is good for twelve months. One-day passes also are sold, typically for $5 each. People caught parking a vehicle that does not display a pass face fines of $50. The passes are required at most popular trailheads in areas managed by the U.S. Forest Service and at North Cascades National Park.

Information on which trailheads require the Northwest Forest Pass is available on the Internet at *www.fs.fed.us/r6/feedemo/welcome.html*. If you cannot log on, follow this simple rule: If you want to hike a specific trail, it is probably popular enough to require a pass, so you will have to buy one. Passes are not available at trailheads but can be purchased in advance at outdoor shops, ranger stations, stores in areas close to wilderness sites, or online. Experienced hikers usually buy trailhead passes long before their hikes. On some occasions, the stores and ranger stations will not be open when you arrive or will not have passes in stock.

If a trail passes through a protected wilderness area, hikers will likely be asked to self-register at the trailhead. This is required for backpackers planning overnight visits and for hikers on short day trips. Registration does not cost anything—yet.

Mount Rainier rises above the horizon of Blankenship Meadows.
(Photo by Skip Card)

Day hikers visiting Mount Rainier or Olympic National Parks need not register, but overnight camping inside either national park requires a wilderness permit, available at most park ranger stations. Most campsites are popular, most can hold just so many people, and tent spots in some sites are reserved months in advance. Backpackers who do not get to the ranger station early during peak summer months will likely find they are out of luck.

The rules governing fees and outdoor uses change frequently. For the latest information, call the phone numbers listed in the Information section for each hike.

Wilderness Ethics

The Northwest's wilderness is not what it used to be. What people a century ago viewed as a raw and rugged land is now seen as a place that has a fragile susceptibility to careless human acts. Practices once common in Washington's backcountry—large campfires, sprawling camps, open trash pits, wandering tromps through alpine meadows, and temporary beds made out of boughs hacked from the nearest fir tree—have been curtailed as population has increased and wilderness areas have become less remote. Today's hikers and backpackers are urged to behave respectfully during their temporary visits into the state's wild areas and to follow rules designed to leave few, if any, lasting impacts.

Those who follow the trails recommended in this book are urged to obey a progressive wilderness ethic designed to respect the environment and to preserve backcountry areas for future generations. We urge all hikers and backpackers to adhere to the following:

■ Avoid making campfires, which scar the soil, create unsightly debris, and often strip campsites bare of any loose wood. Campfires also can easily spread out of control, leading to blazes that destroy vast tracts of forest and wilderness habitat.

■ If you simply have to make a campfire, keep it small. Build fires only in established fire rings and only where fires are legally permitted and can be safely controlled. Burn only dead or downed wood, and never cut live trees for fuel. Douse the fire, and make sure it is out before leaving your camp. Use stoves, not fires, for cooking.

■ Do not pick wildflowers, do not uproot plants, and do not disturb rocks or other natural features.

■ Visualize potential impacts when selecting a campsite, and camp in spots that will not be harmed by your presence. When packing up your camp, restore the site to its previous condition.

■ Hang food out of the reach of animals. Suspend it at least 10 feet off the ground and at least 4 feet from the trunk of the nearest tree. Making food unobtainable to raccoons, bears, and other animals keeps your food supply safe and discourages unnatural behavior in the animals.

■ Leave pets at home. Many areas, particularly national parks, do not allow dogs to roam anywhere, including parking lots, even when on a leash.

■ Use established backcountry toilets where available. If none is available in a forested area, bury human waste in a hole dug 6 to 8 inches deep, at least 200 feet from all water sources, and far from all campsites. Pack out and *do not bury* toilet paper, facial tissue, or any scented paper.

■ If traveling on snow, bag, tightly seal, pack out, and properly dispose of all waste.

■ If crossing private property, always show respect for landowners' rights. On public property, obey all posted rules and obtain all necessary permits.

Above all, hikers are urged to be courteous, respectful and, when necessary, helpful to others they meet on the trail or at established camps. Say a friendly hello when meeting fellow travelers in the wilderness. Step aside in narrow areas to let others pass. Offer help if someone seems lost or unsure of the route. Share information about trail conditions, weather, or scenic viewpoints. Be particularly respectful when camping within earshot of another party, and keep your voices low when others may be trying to sleep. Share food and water with those who did not bring enough, and offer medical supplies or assistance to anyone who appears injured.

And, if you are having a wonderful time exploring a hike in a sunny rain shadow area that you did not know existed until you read about it in this book, tell everyone who sent you.

A Note About Safety

Safety is an important concern in all outdoor activities. No guidebook can alert you to every hazard or anticipate the limitations of every reader. Therefore, the descriptions of roads, trails, routes, and natural features in this book are not representations that a particular place or excursion will be safe for your party. When you follow any of the routes described in this book, you assume responsibility for your own safety. Under normal conditions, such excursions require the usual attention to traffic, road and trail conditions, weather, terrain, the capabilities of your party, and other factors. Because many of the lands in this book are subject to development and/or change of ownership, conditions may have changed since this book was written that make your use of some of these routes unwise. Always check for current conditions, obey posted private property signs, and avoid confrontations with property owners or managers. Keeping informed on current conditions and exercising common sense are the keys to a safe, enjoyable outing.

The Mountaineers Books

Facing page: The view from Mount Constitution. (Photo by Skip Card)

OLYMPICS RAIN SHADOW

S ome mental health experts see a three-way correlation between severe depression, suicide, and miserable, wet weather. No surprise, then, that suicide rates in the Pacific Northwest are higher than the national average. If you want really depressing weather statistics, look up the winter rainfall totals on Washington's Olympic Peninsula. The rainfall record for the soggy coastal town of Forks is 29.2 inches in November and 27.8 inches in December. The Quinault Ranger Station at the southern end of the Olympic rain forest once recorded 12 inches of rain in *one day*.

These are depressing numbers if you are a fair-weather hiker. And they beg this question: Given such rainfall totals, how can anyone suggest dry hikes so close to the Olympic Mountains?

The answer lies in the way the Olympics block the rain. During the winter, strong southwest winds can pile drenching rain and heavy snow on the mountains' southwest slopes, but Sequim and the San Juan Islands benefit from drier downslope winds. The east slopes of the Olympics do not benefit from this pattern to the same extent in winter, but they often see a rain shadow effect in summer during a weak marine push. Weak westerly winds can bring light drizzle to the Pacific coast and west slopes of the Olympics, while portions of the east slopes 5000 feet and higher will bask in sun.

Distance also is key. The suggested hikes in the Olympic rain shadow are a good distance away from the soggy rain forest. They also receive varying amounts of rain. The driest hike without question is Dungeness Spit, a 5-mile strip of sand close to Sequim. (A note for readers from outside the region: "Sequim" looks like "See-kwim" but is properly pronounced "Skwim.") Sequim averages 16.74 inches of rain a year, and in 1944 the city received just 10 inches—desert conditions, meteorologically speaking. Sequim's tourism-minded city council even passed a law against bad weather: Ordinance 95.009, Section 2.1, prohibits "weather conditions that are detrimental to the enjoyment of activities within the city." Most summers, nature obeys.

Another worthy rain shadow lies around the San Juan Islands and the areas near Whidbey Island. Many of these spots receive about half the rainfall of Seattle. Less dry—but still drier than the surrounding area—is the region around the eastern slopes of the Olympics close to Hood Canal. Hikers take a few more weather risks here. (Remember, we promise only the statistical likelihood of staying dry. Unlike elected officials in Sequim, we have no legal authority to guarantee sun.)

All rain shadow bets are off during the wet season, typically from November through March. The region around Dungeness Spit can actually get some significant snow during December as cold air sweeps in from the Fraser River Valley in Canada. In a single day, 10 inches of snow can fall on the Sequim foothills. There ought to be a law.

MOUNT CONSTITUTION

Distance ■	**6.9 miles (loop)**
Hiking time ■	3 to 4 hours
Starting elevation ■	920 feet
High point ■	2409 feet
Hikable ■	Early spring through late fall
Maps ■	USGS Mount Constitution. Free trail maps available at Moran State Park
Information ■	Moran State Park, Orcas Island, 360-376-2326

Most sightseers drive their vehicles to the top of 2409-foot Mount Constitution, highest point in the San Juan Islands archipelago. Shame on them. Cars put people within an easy walk of the popular peak's stone observation tower, but visitors who focus solely on the summit miss their chance to stroll through the spectacular forests and lakes of scenic Moran State Park—and the paths are always less crowded than the pavement.

The journey up the mountain begins with a sea voyage, since most hikers will reach Orcas Island by way of a Washington state ferry that ships out of Anacortes. Ferry schedules change with the seasons; for current schedules and fares call the ferry's information line at 800-843-3779 or visit the state Department of Transportation website at *www.wsdot.wa.gov*. Reservations are recommended for travel during peak times, and drivers are urged to arrive an hour before a ferry's scheduled departure.

Disembark at Orcas Village and follow the traffic north along Orcas Road, one of several streets that collectively make up the U-shaped Horseshoe Highway. Curve around the island and follow signs to Moran State Park until, 13.6 miles from the ferry dock, you drive under the crescent-shaped arch that marks the park entrance. Drive another 1.3 miles, past Cascade

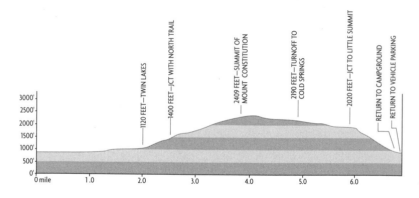

Lake, and turn left on Mount Constitution Road (listed on many maps as "Mountain Road"). Go 1 mile and turn right at the sign to Mountain Lake. Drive 0.3 mile to Mountain Lake Campground, then another 0.2 mile on a gravel road to the small parking area at the Mountain Lake Landing boat launch. (If this small lot is full of vehicles, drive back to the campground and park near the picnic shelter. The hike wraps up there, anyway.) The trailhead is on the north side of the Mountain Lake Landing parking lot.

The 3.4-mile hike to the summit of Mount Constitution begins with a

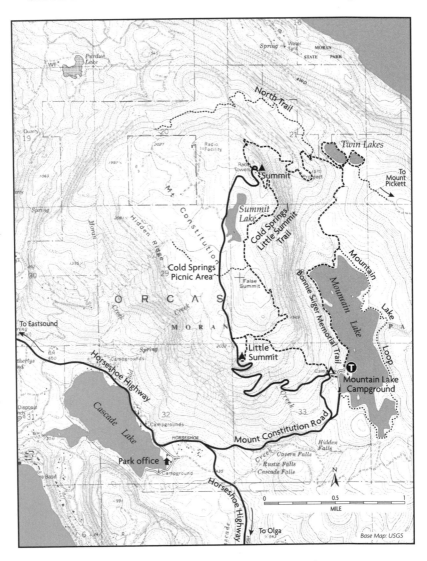

Mount Baker on the horizon, as seen from Mount Constitution.
(Photo by Skip Card)

level stroll along Mountain Lake's rocky, log-strewn shoreline on a wide path known as the Bonnie Sliger Memorial Trail. After 1.3 miles, at a junction at the end of the lake, veer north to begin 0.8 mile of gentle uphill grade to Twin Lakes. Trails here are littered with the needles and tinder of evergreens, and hikers hear birdsong and the gurgle of creeks as they breathe in the scent of cedar tinged with the salt of sea breezes.

Loop trails encircle the tiny Twin Lakes, elevation 1120 feet, but the path to Mount Constitution veers left and immediately begins gaining elevation in earnest. At 0.3 mile beyond the lakes, head straight at the junction with the North Trail and begin a series of steep switchbacks and wide curves. The 1.5-mile trail—and any solitude or silence—ends at the Mount Constitution parking lot, where hikers join the drive-in crowd for the final few uphill steps to the summit.

Mount Constitution is crowned by a sandstone observation tower with wood timbers and iron supports. The tower was designed by architect Ellsworth Storey to resemble twelfth-century watchtowers in Europe's Caucasus Mountains. It was constructed in 1936 by Depression-era workers in the Civilian Conservation Corps, who also built many of Moran State Park's roads, bridges, and trails. At the base of the tower, a display explains how former Seattle Mayor Robert Moran donated the original 2731 acres that later became Moran State Park.

Sweeping views can be had from the tower or the sloping viewing area just below it. Mount Baker and the jagged Twin Sisters loom largest on the eastern horizon, but on clear days visitors can see south down the Cascade Mountains as far as Mount Rainier. Some of the San Juan Islands are visible, such as Cypress and Lummi, sitting green amid the blue of Rosario Strait and nearby waterways.

Hikers who get their fill of the views can return along their original route or can cozy up to a friendly motorist and bum a ride. A more scenic option, however, is to locate the trailhead behind the restrooms and descend back to Mountain Lake via the Cold Springs/Little Summit Trail. The undulating route begins amid dense woods but soon opens onto a 0.5-mile-long ridge with excellent views to the east. Hikers stay left for 1 mile to descend from the summit and to avoid the turnoff to Cold Springs—a surprisingly forlorn picnic area considering that virtually every trail sign points there. After a ridge-skirting mile offering bird's-eye views of Mountain Lake, hikers hit the junction to Little Summit. This quiet, 2020-foot viewpoint has a fraction of the crowds (and the views) of Mount Constitution, but it makes a good rest stop worth a detour before the final descent.

The last 0.8 mile back to Mountain Lake heads steeply down a switch-backing path through heavy stands of western hemlock and Douglas fir. The trail ends at the Mountain Lake Campground picnic shelter, leaving hikers a brief 0.2-mile walk on gravel road back to their vehicles at the boat launch. Those who are not camping at Moran or staying at an Orcas Island inn should schedule their day to allow time to catch a ferry off the island.

2 ┊ FIDALGO HEAD LOOP

Distance ■	**2.6 miles (round trip)**
Hiking time ■	1.5 hours
Starting elevation ■	Sea level
High point ■	150 feet
Hikable ■	Year-round
Maps ■	USGS Deception Pass and Cypress Island (trails not shown)
Information ■	City of Anacortes Parks and Recreation Department, 360-293-1918

Remember hikes you took as a kid? They probably occurred back when "camping" involved an aluminum trailer instead of a North Face tent, and a "hike" was an hour of joyful exploration rather than a three-day bushwhack. Yet some avid hikers never lose an appreciation for short loop trails where a map (even if one existed) would be far less useful than follow-your-nose common sense, and some longtime hikers who have children of their own are looking for a short path with enough scene changes and challenge to hold short attention spans. Either group—as well as anyone who missed

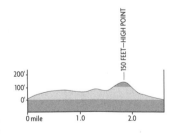

the San Juan Islands ferry—should enjoy the loop trail around Washington Park on Fidalgo Head.

Follow Highway 20 Spur west into Anacortes, turn right onto Commercial Avenue, then turn left at the light onto 12th Street, following signs to "Highway 20 Spur/San Juan Ferry." Follow the ferry traffic for 3 miles, then veer left onto Sunset Avenue. Follow Sunset for 0.6 mile to the Washington Park entrance. Parking is available at the beach area, the picnic area, and in a day-use lot near the parking area for boat trailers. If camping, continue past the boat launch toward the loop road and veer left into the campground.

Washington Park, owned and operated by the City of Anacortes, is an unadvertised gem that occupies 220 acres on picturesque Fidalgo Head, a bulb of land jutting into Rosario Strait. Saltwater surrounds the park on three sides, and a loop road runs near the scenic shoreline, encircling the large campground. The Fidalgo Head Loop Trail skirts the shoreline, often dropping down to the water's edge and even joining the road in spots where steep beach bluffs cannot support a trail.

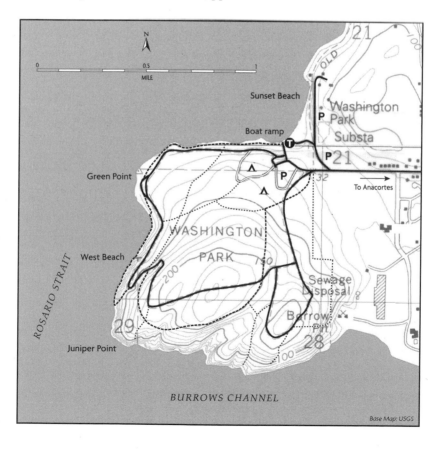

The waters of Burrows Channel as seen from the trail that loops around Fidalgo Head. (Photo by Skip Card)

The Fidalgo Head trailhead sits at the edge of the woods beside the Sunset Beach picnic area near the boat ramp. A sign notes the trail is "1.6 miles," but since the loop is a least a mile longer, it is anyone's guess what this mileage refers to. Similarly confusing signs elsewhere in the park seem to list the distances to key junctions, yet so many intersections exist amid the park's official and unofficial trails that hikers seeking a precise route are sure to become frustrated. Most hikers learn to follow the widest path that runs parallel to the shore. If seriously confused or lost, simply head inland to join the road.

From Sunset Beach, the trail runs amid brushy foliage for about 0.3 mile to Green Point, a scenic picnic area where park workers are restoring native vegetation. Those who stop to watch the shipping traffic are asked to stay out of fenced-off areas where plants such as shooting stars are again taking root. About 0.1 mile farther, hikers can descend concrete stairs to the rocks and sand of West Beach, a popular spot for low-tide exploration. Unofficial paths at the far end of the beach let capable hikers scramble off the beach and up a low bluff; small children or anyone unsure of their abilities should head back up the stairs and walk along the road.

The coastline becomes steeper and more craggy as the trail wraps around Fidalgo Head to face Burrows Channel, the swift-moving strait that separates Washington Park from Burrows Island. Hikers at times might find themselves tiptoeing along what seems to be little more than a goat track through coarse grass and red soil. In other places, the trails are broad paths among mature trees or narrow channels hacked through thick foliage.

As they pick their way among the paths, hikers should be alert to some of the beautiful blossoms that grow in the park. Favorites that appear in spring include the calypso orchid, chocolate lily, and fawn lily.

Wrong turns can become common near the end of the loop as hikers encounter junctions with trails that snake into the park from neighborhoods near Skyline Marina. Those who find themselves momentarily lost can retrace their steps, ask directions from a friendly local, or head inland to find the loop road. Ultimately, the trail deposits hikers back on the loop road, about a couple hundred yards from the junction with the main drive where they may complete the loop with a walk along the road back to their vehicles.

3 DUNGENESS SPIT

Distance ■	**10 miles (round trip)**
Hiking time ■	4 to 5 hours
Starting elevation ■	120 feet
High point ■	120 feet
Hikable ■	Year-round, although some areas are difficult to reach during winter high tides
Maps ■	USGS Dungeness; U.S. Fish & Wildlife Service maps are available at the trailhead
Information ■	Dungeness National Wildlife Refuge, 360-457-8451

Washington's scenic shoreline would be hiker heaven were it not for two things: drenching coastal rainfall and state laws that let private parties own tidelands. As it is, shoreline hikers who are not getting soaked often get threatened with trespassing. However, both problems evaporate in the relatively dry climate of Dungeness Spit, a 5-mile-long sweep of sand, rock, and driftwood that is the keystone of the federal Dungeness National Wildlife Refuge. The spit typically gets just under 17 inches of rain each year, although more than half of that falls between November and February. Weather conditions at the spit are rarely calm and balmy, but the terrain offers relatively dry spring and summer hiking with excellent opportunities to view waterfowl and other wildlife.

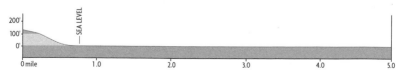

To reach Dungeness Spit, follow US 101 a few miles west of Sequim and turn north on Kitchen-Dick Road, following signs to Dungeness National Wildlife Refuge and Dungeness Recreation Area. Follow Kitchen-Dick for 3 miles until the road turns right and becomes Lotzgesell Road, then turn left into the refuge on Voice of America Road. The Dungeness Spit trailhead is 1 mile up the road, past the horse trails, picnic areas, and campground. Park in the large parking lot, where restrooms and water are available. The wildlife refuge is open from sunrise until dusk and charges hikers a fee, currently $3 per family. Pay envelopes are provided at the trailhead, and exact change is required. Pets, guns, kites, fires, and camping are not permitted.

From the trailhead, a wide dirt trail descends 0.5 mile through dense coastal forest to the shoreline. Hikers should be sure to pause at one of several hillside overlooks to view the vast spit, formed continually as the silt from eroding coastal bluffs is transported and deposited by the Strait of Juan de Fuca's strong currents. Oceanographers claim no other natural sand spit in the world reaches this length.

Once on the beach, spit visitors are typically required to stay on the surf-splashed northern shore that faces the strait. Hiking is prohibited on the sheltered south side so nesting birds and other animals will not be disturbed. Many visitors leisurely wander the shoreline enjoying crashing waves and salt-scented sea breezes. Others bring binoculars to spy on the spit's vast collection of wildlife. More than 250 bird species live on or stop by Dungeness Spit, and signs along the upper trail list the species

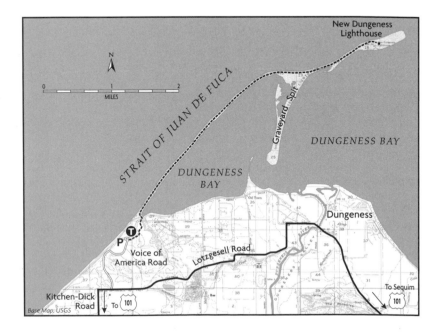

Waves roll up on the shores of Dungeness Spit. (Photo by Alan L. Bauer)

most recently spotted. Visitors also might see eight species of marine mammals—particularly harbor seals—and forty-one species of land mammals, such as weasels, skunks, and black-tailed deer.

Serious hikers head along the shoreline toward the tip of the spit and the New Dungeness Lighthouse. If possible, plan your visit to coincide with outgoing tides, since the wet, wave-washed tidelands afford better footing than the dry sand and drift logs at the spit's crest. Hikers marching with head-down concentration often see an assortment of odds and ends that washed in from the Pacific Ocean. Those looking up to scan the horizon typically spot Asia-bound ships or the heads of curious harbor seals bobbing in the kelp beds beyond the surf.

After 3 miles of spit walking, hikers can approach the crest of Dungeness

Spit and look south over an interior arm known as Graveyard Spit. This sandy offshoot earned its name after an 1868 massacre in which eighteen Tsimshian Indians camped on the site were killed by rival S'Klallams.

Another 1.5 miles brings hikers to the manicured grounds of the New Dungeness Lighthouse, built in 1857 at what was then the tip of the spit. Sand continues to pile up on the spit, increasing its length by about 15 feet a year, but the 0.5-mile stretch beyond the lighthouse is closed to hikers so a colony of harbor seals can sunbathe unmolested.

New Dungeness Lighthouse spent more than a century waving ships away from the protruding shore before new navigational technology made staffing the light unnecessary. Due to be boarded up, the lighthouse was saved by citizen volunteers who formed the New Dungeness Chapter of the U.S. Lighthouse Society. Members today keep watch over the lighthouse and its nearby keeper's cottage and conduct tours up the 63-foot light tower, from which visitors can gaze across the strait to Victoria, B.C. Tours are free, but donations are gladly accepted.

Most hikers relax amid the light station's mowed grass and picnic tables to enjoy a snack and a brief rest before beginning the return journey. The trip often begins with a rude surprise: Prevailing north and west winds that pushed at hikers' backs during the trip out now hit them square in the face during the walk back to the vehicle.

4 ┆ DEER PARK TO OBSTRUCTION POINT

Distance ■	7.5 miles (one way), 15 miles (round trip)
Hiking time ■	3.5 hours (one way)
Starting elevations ■	5200 feet at Deer Park, 6140 feet at Obstruction Point
High point ■	6540 feet (Elk Mountain, 6779 feet)
Open and hikable ■	Mid-July to October
Maps ■	Green Trails 135 Mount Angeles; USGS Maiden Peak and Mount Angeles; Custom Correct Gray Wolf/ Dosewallips and Hurricane Ridge
Information ■	Wilderness Information Center, Olympic National Park, 360-565-3100

Few trails other than the ridgeline path skirting three peaks between Deer Park and Obstruction Point offer such a stunning combination of blue sea and sweeping mountain views. The trade-off is distance; hikers who cannot find a way to leave a vehicle at both ends of this hike face a daunting round trip that can stretch up to 15 miles. Hikers can start at either end of the ridge trail. Those who begin at Obstruction Point reach the highest viewpoint much sooner and have the option of detouring on nearby paths. Hikers who start at more obscure Deer Park get a fuller picture of the region, since their path begins amid a forested hillside that the Obstruction Point crowd usually never reaches. Deer Park also is closer to metropolitan centers, such as Seattle.

The easy-to-find Obstruction Point trailhead sits at the end of 8-mile-long Obstruction Point Road, which starts at the Hurricane Ridge Visitor Center. To reach the Deer Park trailhead, turn off US 101 at Deer Park Road east of Port Angeles. Drive south 9.1 miles on a paved road that narrows as it approaches the boundary of Olympic National Park, then abruptly turns to gravel and dirt. Another 8.1 miles of narrow road with hairpin turns and sheer drop-offs (unsuitable for trailers or drivers suffering vertigo) lead to a small parking area near the Deer Park Ranger Station.

Starting from the Deer Park trailhead, the trail begins at 5200 feet but loses 270 feet in the first 0.5 mile, after which hikers begin a long but rarely steep uphill journey through sparse forest. Views improve as hikers break out of the trees and head toward 5390-foot Green Mountain. The trail skirts just to the south of this grassy summit, then tracks east and then south along a ridge that sneaks below 6434-foot Maiden Peak. By this point, hikers have traveled 3.8 miles, and many choose to drink in the excellent views here and turn back.

Those who continue follow a sometimes tricky path that drops about 300 feet in 0.7 mile to Roaring Winds Camp, a rest stop set at 5975 feet in a breeze-battered gap. Backpackers planning an overnight stay must obtain wilderness permits. Resuming their uphill course, hikers follow an often exposed path that snakes up and across the long ridge leading to Elk Mountain. Hikers should take care not to be so distracted by the stunning range of peaks to the south that they lose their footing on the steep slope and tumble down to Grand Creek.

About 5.5 miles from Deer Park, the trail tops out at a 6540-foot intersection

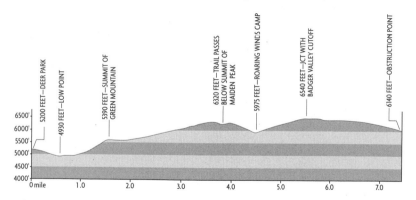

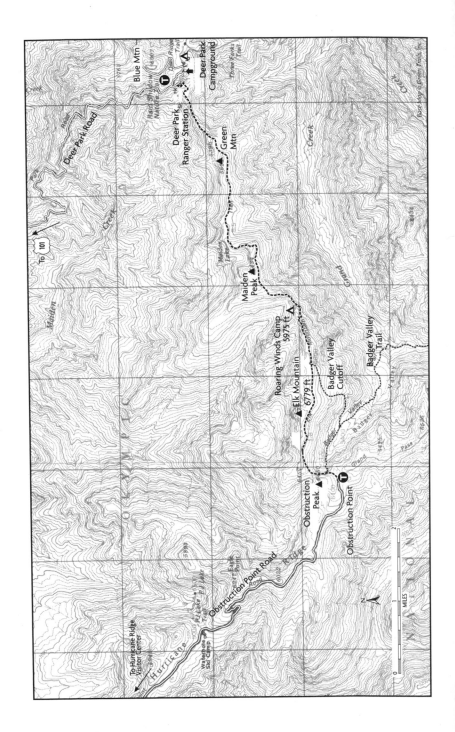

The trail from Deer Park to Obstruction Point. (Photo by Skip Card)

with an unmaintained cutoff path down to Badger Valley. Many hikers step off the trail here and walk gently uphill to Elk Mountain's broad 6779-foot summit, which offers a 360-degree sweep of sea and snowcapped peaks. Pesky bugs also seem to like the views; lunch may be eaten on Elk Mountain's summit, but it is rarely enjoyed.

Round-trip hikers who want to brag that they completed the entire route can walk the mostly downhill 2 miles to the parking lot at 6140-foot Obstruction Point before turning around and retracing their steps. Most choose merely to find a good resting spot and gaze out at all the natural splendor before beginning their return.

5 MOUNT TOWNSEND

Distance ■	10.2 miles (round trip)
Hiking time ■	4 to 5 hours
Starting elevation ■	2840 feet
High point ■	6280 feet
Hikable ■	June through October
Maps ■	Green Trails 136 Tyler Peak; USGS Mount Townsend; Custom Correct Buckhorn Wilderness
Information ■	Quilcene Ranger Station, Olympic National Forest, 360-765-2200

Few peaks offer such superb views as Mount Townsend, a serene throne from which hikers can take in a spectacular sweep of scenery ranging from deep seas to soaring mountaintops. The cost of the views is a steady uphill hike that averages a 20 percent grade.

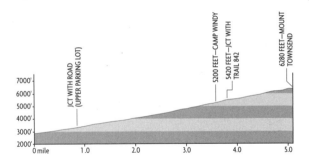

From US 101, head northwest on Penny Creek Road near the Quilcene National Fish Hatchery, just 1 mile south of the Quilcene Ranger Station. Veer left at 1.5 miles, when pavement temporarily gives way to gravel, and follow signs to Forest Service Road (FS) 27, a one-lane paved road with occasional wide spots and several distracting turnoffs. Stay on FS 27, following signs to Mount Townsend. About 14 miles from the highway, turn left onto FS 2760 at a sign to the Mount Townsend Trail. The trailhead is designated by a sign near a small parking area 0.8 mile down the gravel road.

(For a shorter hike, continue on FS 27 another 1 mile past the intersection with FS 2760, turn left at the hairpin turn onto a primitive dead-end service road, and drive 0.8 mile to a small parking lot at the road's end.)

From the lower trailhead, elevation 2840 feet, Mount Townsend Trail 839

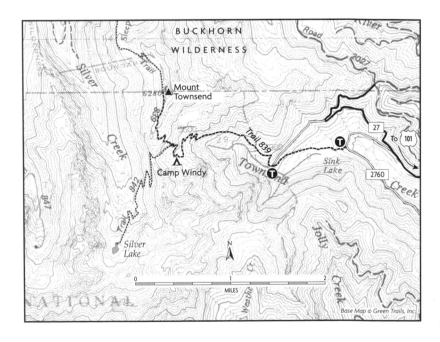

Mount Townsend's rocky summit offers excellent views west toward Puget Sound. (Photo by Skip Card)

follows a gentle path that passes tiny Sink Lake and a small shelter. The upper parking lot appears in 0.9 mile, and the trail begins switchbacking up steeper terrain. Towering wild rhododendron and vine maple crowd the densely forested path for the next mile but grow more sparse about the time hikers cross the boundary into the Buckhorn Wilderness.

Continuing higher, hikers eventually pass through hillside flower meadows and watch tall, thick-trunked lowland trees give way to stunted subalpine varieties. Views improve with each uphill step, and eventually the curve of Hood Canal comes into view. At about 2.7 miles from the upper parking lot is a short detour to Camp Windy, elevation 5200 feet. The junction with Trail 842 to Silver Lake is 0.2 mile farther.

Staying right at the junction, hikers climb to about 6020 feet, crest a ridge, and get their first jaw-dropping view of the steep, craggy peaks west of Silver Creek. Mount Townsend's broad summit rises to the north, about 1.3 miles from the junction. Hikers reach the summit via a faint footpath that veers from the main trail.

On sunny weekends, the rocks and meadow grass of Townsend's summit are often crowded with hikers eating lunch while they enjoy the 360-degree view. On one side, Olympic peaks such as Mount Baldy and Tyler Peak poke above forested hillsides that spill down to dark river valleys. At sea level sit Sequim Bay, Discovery Bay, Hood Canal, and the Strait of Juan de Fuca. The snowy summits of Mount Baker, Mount Rainier, and other Cascade peaks loom to the east, rising above the smog of lowland cities.

6 BUCKHORN MOUNTAIN

Distance ■	**12.4 miles (round trip)**
Hiking time ■	5 to 6 hours
Starting elevation ■	2480 feet
High point ■	6988 feet
Hikable ■	Late June to early November
Maps ■	Green Trails 136 Tyler Peak; USGS Mount Townsend; Custom Correct Buckhorn Wilderness (esp. for accurate mileage)
Information ■	Quilcene Ranger Station, Olympic National Forest, 360-765-2200

The views from this craggy perch are worth the long stretch of steady up-hill hiking that begins in dense and sometimes drippy forest but ultimately makes its way up into classic rain shadow terrain.

Buckhorn Mountain is accessible from Big Quilcene Trail 833. To reach the trailhead, follow US 101 and turn northwest on Penny Creek Road near the Quilcene National Fish Hatchery near the Big Quilcene River, about 1 mile from the Quilcene Ranger Station. Veer left at 1.5 miles, when pavement temporarily gives way to gravel, and follow signs to Forest Service Road (FS) 27, a one-lane paved road. Stay on FS 27, past the turnoff to the Lower Big Quilcene Trail. Turn left at the sign to the upper trail onto FS 2750 and drive 4.5 miles to the upper trailhead.

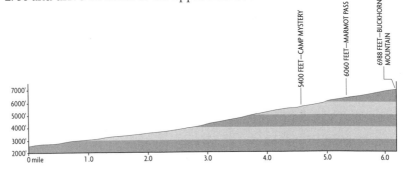

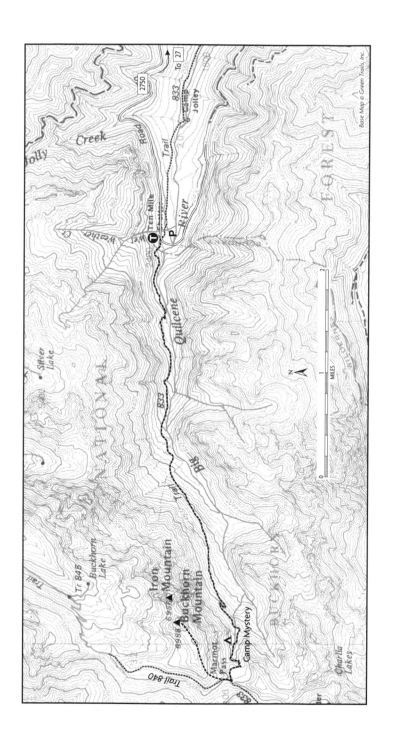

Base Map © Green Trails, Inc.

Approaching the summit of Buckhorn Mountain. (Photo by Skip Card)

For the first 2.5 miles, Trail 833 runs through thick forest close to the Big Quilcene River, then it leaves the riverbed (and the last reliably flowing water) and steadily gains elevation. Views improve as hikers work their way up and out of the trees to catch glimpses of the jagged peaks rising from the south side of the river valley. On the north side, equally impressive crags seem to loom directly above the trail.

After 4.6 miles, the trail flattens momentarily as it snakes past campsites at Camp Mystery, elevation 5400 feet. Sharp-eyed hikers might find some springs with flowing water, but backpackers planning to camp here should play it safe and haul in their own water supply.

Beyond this tempting rest stop, the trail snakes through a sheltered meadow as it ascends the final 660 feet to Marmot Pass, a trail junction offering sweeping views to the west. Hikers pooped after covering 5.3 uphill miles can turn back here content with the scenery.

For an even better vantage point, turn right onto Trail 840 to Copper Creek, then quickly veer off the trail onto the faint uphill track leading 0.9 mile up to 6988-foot Buckhorn Mountain. The craggy rocks of Buckhorn and nearby 6956-foot Iron Mountain offer excellent places to rest, eat a snack, and take in views stretching from the Strait of Juan de Fuca in the north to various summits along the eastern horizon. To the south, about 4 miles from Buckhorn as the crow flies, stands 7743-foot Mount Constance and nearby 7300-foot Warrior Peak.

1 MOUNT ELLINOR

Distance ▪	**3.2 miles from upper trailhead (round trip), 6.4 miles from lower trailhead (round trip)**
Hiking time ▪	2 hours from upper trailhead, 3 to 4 hours from lower trailhead
Starting elevation ▪	3520 feet at upper trailhead, 2560 feet at lower trailhead
High point ▪	5944 feet
Hikable ▪	July through October
Maps ▪	Green Trails 167 Mount Steel and 168 The Brothers; USGS Mount Skokomish; Custom Correct Mount Skokomish/Lake Cushman
Information ▪	Hood Canal Ranger Station, Olympic National Forest, 360-877-5254

Stunning views from one of the best vantage points in the state make the trail to Mount Ellinor one of the most popular in the Olympics. The peak's popularity has only grown since recent trail improvements converted tricky traverses into manageable pathways. Expect scenery, not solitude.

Hikers can choose a long or short route to Ellinor's summit. To reach the trailheads, take US 101 to Hoodsport and turn west onto State Route 119 (Lake Cushman Road), following signs to the Cushman/Staircase Recreation Area. Follow the road 9 miles to where the pavement ends and turn

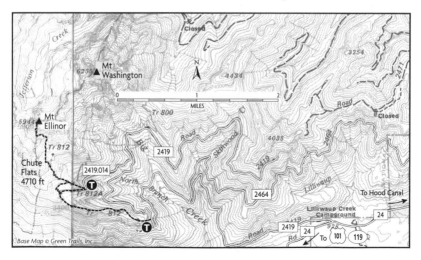

Base Map © Green Trails, Inc.

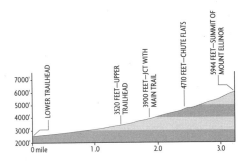

right at the junction with Staircase Road (also known as Forest Service Road 24). Drive 1.5 miles, then hook sharply left on Forest Service Road (FS) 2419. Watch for signs to the Mount Ellinor Trail. Follow FS 2419 as it heads steeply up the Big Creek drainage. A parking area for the trail's lower trailhead is reached after 5 miles, at 2560 feet elevation.

For a shorter hike, continue on FS 2419 another 1.7 miles, turn left onto FS Spur 2419.014 at the sign to Upper Mount Ellinor Trail, and drive a mile to the dead end. The upper trailhead puts hikers at 3520 feet, about 1000 vertical feet closer to the top of Mount Ellinor.

Hikers who start at the lower trailhead pass through 1.9 uphill miles of pleasant forest until they join the path from the upper trailhead. Then the trail follows a steep mile of steps and switchbacks through thick forest. Some views and a tiny patch of level ground appear around 4710 feet at a decent resting spot known as Chute Flats. Beyond, the soil is sometimes so thin that the trail in places becomes a winding route through boulders marked by a few small red diamond symbols.

Mount Washington seen through the clouds from the summit of Mount Ellinor. (Photo by Skip Card)

Emerging from the boulder field, hikers regain a more obvious trail that traverses steep flower meadows and follows ridges dotted with stunted trees. Views improve with each step as the trail winds the final feet to Mount Ellinor's rocky 5944-foot summit.

Views can be remarkable on clear days. Lake Cushman sits to the south, while just to the north rises 6255-foot Mount Washington. Hood Canal is visible to the east, and to the west stand the many peaks that form the backbone border between the Olympic National Forest and Olympic National Park.

But that is just the immediate vicinity. From atop Ellinor's summit, hikers can see Mount Rainier, Mount Adams, and Mount St. Helens, as well as Olympic giants such as Mount Olympus. Large cities such as Seattle also are often visible; just look for boxy towers peeking out of the brown smog.

Descend the way you came, and be careful not to lose your way amid the boulders.

8 EBEY'S LANDING

Distance ■	**3.7 miles (loop)**
Hiking time ■	2 hours
Starting elevation ■	20 feet
High point ■	260 feet
Hikable ■	Year-round
Map ■	USGS Coupeville
Information ■	Fort Casey State Park, 360-678-4519; Ebey's Landing National Historic Reserve, 360-678-6084

The curving beaches and high bluffs on the kelp-scented west coast of Whidbey Island offer some of the best opportunities in the state for shoreline strolls. The cream of this coastline is Ebey's Landing, a patchwork collection of state park, federal historic reserve, nature preserve, and private land. A popular 3.7-mile loop trail traces the best of bluff and beach, but hikers itching to explore more can stretch their legs for miles to the north and south.

Ebey's Landing is southwest of Coupeville on Whidbey Island, accessible from the north via Anacortes or from the south via the ferry to Mukilteo. Once in Coupeville, turn off State Route 20 onto Ebey Road and drive 1.6 miles to the western shore. A small parking lot sits amid coastal driftwood where Ebey Road makes a hairpin turn south, and overflow parking is available on the road's shoulder a short distance away.

Kiosk displays near the parking area detail the site's history. The coastal

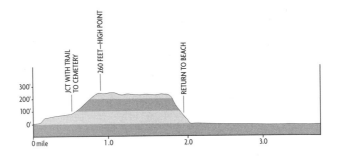

prairie had been a local source of camas bulbs and other plants for centuries before Isaac Ebey arrived in 1850 and started Whidbey Island's first successful farm. Over the next seven years, Ebey also took on the jobs of district attorney, customs collector, territorial delegate, and adjutant general for Washington Territory. His position was lofty enough to attract the unwelcome attention of a band of Haida warriors looking to avenge the death of their chief a year earlier in Port Gamble. In January 1857, Ebey was killed and his head carried north as a trophy—later to be recovered and buried with the rest of his body.

Climb the steps up the bluff and walk northwest along the high bank. In 0.5 mile the path reaches a junction with a 1-mile side trail to Sunnyside Cemetery, site of numerous pioneer graves and the small, wood-frame Davis Blockhouse built in 1855. Many who travel this path hope to spot the rare golden paintbrush, a wildflower that blooms nowhere else in Washington and in only six other sites around the world. (If the cemetery is your destination, it is easily accessible by motor vehicle. Save your hiking time for the beach.)

Beyond the junction, the path steepens as the trail works its way up the seaside bluffs that border the Robert Pratt Preserve. Pratt died in 1999, and in his will he left 147 acres of family farm to The Nature Conservancy. The preserve forms the core of a larger parcel that keeps Ebey's Landing in a semi-natural state rather than pockmarked with condos.

The trail tops out about 260 feet above sea level as hikers trace a sandy crest between a forest of wind-gnarled firs and the grassy slope that drops steeply to the beach. Views are sublime. Port Townsend and Fort Worden sit on the far shore, across the glistening blue waters of Admiralty Inlet, shadowed by craggy peaks in the Olympic Mountains. On clear days, hikers can even see Vancouver Island to the north and Mount Rainier more than a hundred miles to the south. Common Northwest plants such as Oregon grape crowd the trail, but the sun-washed slope is so dry that prickly pear cactus also grows naturally.

Hikers stroll above Perego's Lake, a marshy lagoon named for a local hermit, until the trail forks near the lake's northern tip. The right-hand path leads 0.1 mile to a dead-end viewpoint. The left-hand path heads down

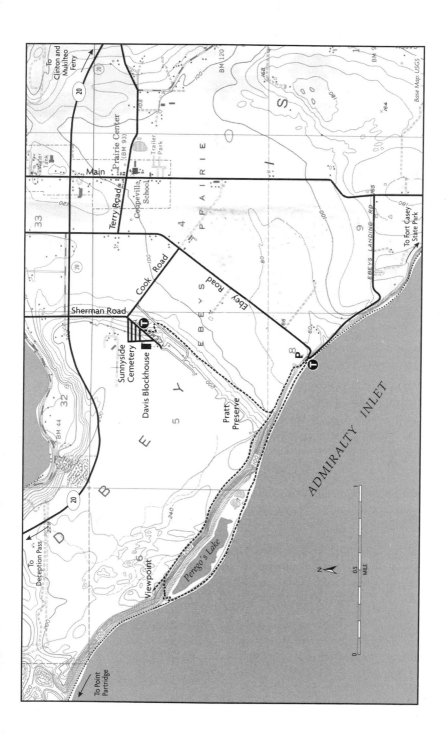

To Clinton and
Mukilteo Ferry

20

20

Prairie Center
(BM 93)

BM 120

Water
Tank

Main

Trailer
Park

Terry Road

Coupeville
School

33

PRAIRIE

EBEY'S

BM 120

168

164

Base Map, USGS

9

To Fort Casey
State Park

EBEYS LANDING RD.

165

180

20

Cook Road

Ebey Road

Sherman Road

T

Sunnyside Cemetery

Davis Blockhouse

Pratt's Preserve

P

T

ADMIRALTY INLET

BM 44

32

E

B

Y

5

To
Deception Pass

20

D

E

B

Y

6

Viewpoint

240

Perego's Lake

N

0.5

MILE

0.5

0

To Point
Partridge

The beach walk at Ebey's Landing is lined with a huge tangle of driftwood logs. (Photo by Alan L. Bauer)

very steeply to the beach along a sand-slippery trail where even surefooted hikers are liable to stumble. Use extreme caution, or consider heading back the way you came along the bluff.

Those who make it down the trail will have walked 1.9 miles by the time they hit the beach. The shoreline path back to the parking lot covers another 1.8 miles of sand, rocks, driftwood, kelp, and whatever jetsam washes ashore at high tide. Shorebirds such as mergansers, goldeneyes, buffleheads, scoters, and the omnipresent seagulls are common sights.

Accessible beach stretches north and south of Ebey's Landing. North of Perego's Lake, hikers can walk 2.2 miles of lonely beach to Point Partridge, part of scenic Fort Ebey State Park. South of the parking lot at the start of this hike, 2.6 miles of shoreline lead to Fort Casey State Park. Both parks feature drive-in campsites, although Fort Casey's campground looks like a gravel parking lot compared to Fort Ebey's tree-shaded grounds. Reservations are recommended for all campers.

NORTH CASCADES
EAST RAIN SHADOW

Major storms can slice right through the North Cascades, a place so wet and mountainous that it has one of the largest concentrations of glaciers in the Lower 48. More than 650 glaciers are currently scouring the rugged slopes of the North Cascades. We counted.

Yet even a place as wild and wet as the North Cascades can have the geographical ingredients to form a rain shadow. Moisture-soaked winds can coat the North Cascades' west slopes with rain and snow, but slopes on the eastern side of the Cascades crest are often far drier. As air descends down the leeward slopes, it picks up warmth and holds moisture better—factors that reduce clouds and rain. Travel just 15 miles east of the crest, and you will see a noticeable drop in precipitation. Go 30 miles, and rainfall drops even more significantly.

Numbers help tell the story. Mount Baker, in the teeth of most storms, gets 230 percent more precipitation than Harts Pass just 60 miles to the east. But hikers do not have to travel all the way to Harts Pass to avoid rain. They can go to Canyon Creek, just east of Ross Lake on State Route 20. Although just 40 miles east of Mount Baker (the official snow capital of the world), the Canyon Creek region is shielded by a virtual fortress of more than thirty peaks that strip moisture from wet southwest winds. When the moisture blows in from the northwest, Canyon Creek gets sheltering assistance from nearby 8905-foot Jack Mountain—as well as 9127-foot Mount Shuksan and 10,785-foot Baker.

A ring of peaks also strips moisture out of the westerly winds that hit Pugh Ridge, a scenic crest just west of Lake Chelan. Before moist air reaches Pugh Ridge, usually it first slams against 10,541-foot Glacier Peak. Any moisture that Glacier misses is often intercepted by the peaks in Chiwawa Ridge and the Entiat Mountains.

Preceding page: Creek and meadow at the base of Pugh Ridge.
(Photo by Skip Card)

9 CANYON CREEK

Distance ■	**11 miles (round trip)**
Hiking time ■	4 to 5 hours
Starting elevation ■	1904 feet
High point ■	2960 feet
Hikable ■	May through October
Maps ■	Green Trails 49 Mount Logan; USGS Crater Mountain and Azurite Peak
Information ■	Methow Valley Wilderness Information Center, Okanogan National Forest, 509-996-4000 (ask about Chancellor Trail 754)

The low elevation and gentle terrain of this scenic river walk above Canyon Creek make it a perfect early-season trek for hikers hoping to shake off winter's cobwebs. Expect to see more canyon than creek, since towering firs hide the rushing waters. Trekking poles will come in handy when crossing the unpredictable creeks or negotiating the washout-prone final leg down to Mill Creek.

The large trailhead parking lot sits just off State Route 20 near milepost 141, about 11 miles east of Colonial Creek Campground and 21 miles east of Newhalem. A restroom is available, and on-site registration is required.

Trail 754, officially known as Chancellor Trail in memory of the abandoned mining town 9 miles east, begins on a well-worn route shared by several paths. Head along Granite Creek, cross the bridge, double back, then look for the easy-to-miss right turn where a sign points to Chancellor. (Hikers who reach another bridge have missed the turn and are heading toward the Jackita Ridge Trail.)

The trail makes a few steep switchbacks to rise over the low ridge and then settles in along a path carved from the steep hillside above Canyon Creek. Although views of the creek are obscured, the melody of crashing water is a constant accompaniment.

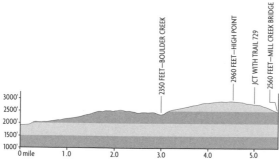

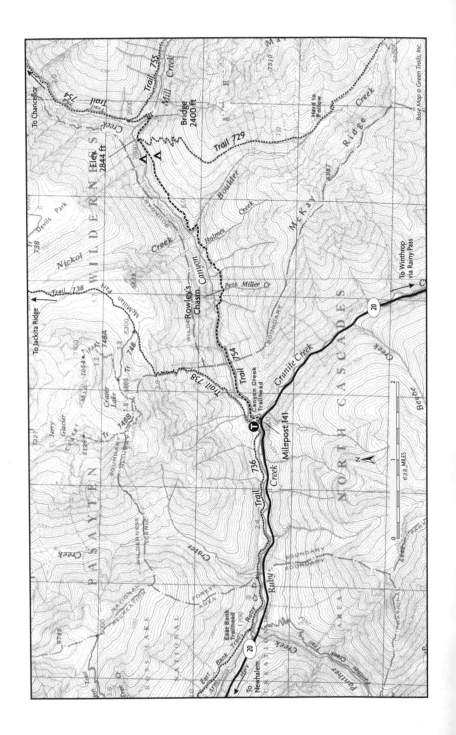

The trail rises steadily and, around 2400 feet elevation, reaches the first of six creeks that cross the path in either a trickle or torrent, depending on the season. Shortly beyond is an abandoned side trail down to Rowley's Chasm, a detour that honors prospector Jack Rowley whose discovery of gold along Canyon Creek in 1879 sparked a rush to the area. (Jack Mountain also honors Rowley, and a creek and pass bear the name of the "Hidden Hand" that he claimed guided him to his pay dirt.)

Good views arrive a bit later as the trail bends toward Pete Miller Creek. Beyond the creek, the trail rises to its cruising altitude of about 2600 feet. This elevation is more or less maintained until just past Holmes Creek when the trail switchbacks down to cross Boulder Creek, the first creek big enough to merit a log footbridge.

The trail rises after this crossing for a long stretch of pleasant uphill walking through shaded forest and green ground cover. Good campsites near a small rocky seep appear about 4.4 miles from the trailhead, just 0.6 mile before a junction with Trail 729.

Beyond the junction, Trail 754 descends a slide-prone zigzag to Mill Creek and its aging wooden bridge. The bleached wood, rushing river, and (most of all) ample sunshine make this crossing a popular rest stop and a worthy turnaround point. Round-trip distance from here measures 11 miles.

Hikers with extra energy and curiosity can switchback up the far side of Mill Creek, along a steep and often overgrown path. Trail 754 skirts an old burn, passes chunks of rusting mill machinery and, after 0.5 mile, reaches a viewpoint where hikers can gaze west down Canyon Creek toward 8347-foot Snowfield Peak.

A ruffled grouse crosses the Canyon Creek Trail. (Photo by Alan L. Bauer)

10 Gold Ridge Tarn

Distance ■	**15 miles (round trip)**
Hiking time ■	2 days
Starting elevation ■	6900 feet
High point ■	6945 feet
Hikable ■	August through early October
Maps ■	Green Trails 18 Pasayten Peak and 50 Washington Pass; USGS Pasayten Peak
Information ■	Methow Valley Visitor Center, Okanogan National Forest, 509-996-4000

This out-of-the-way journey to a scenic mountain lake requires good off-trail routefinding skills and good timing. Arrive too early, and the approach route might be covered in snow. Arrive too late, and winter storms could strike. Still, backpackers who scramble their way up to this isolated jewel in late summer or early autumn will earn the rewards of fall colors, late-blooming wildflowers, and spectacular mountain scenery.

To reach the trailhead, follow State Route 20 to Mazama, 16 miles west of Winthrop. Follow Lost River Road (Forest Service Road 1183) to the northwest, and stay on it when it turns to gravel and becomes Forest Service Road (FS) 5400. Drive slowly and carefully along this narrow road until, 20 miles from Mazama, you reach Harts Pass, site of some primitive car camp spots. From Harts Pass, go right on FS 600, drive another 1.5 miles and park at a place identified on maps as Slate Pass, starting points for Trails 498 and 575.

The 6900-foot trailhead will often be covered in snow until late in the season, but the snow is usually easy to cross. Hikers who arrive in late September or early October will miss the snow and be treated to an autumn display of larch needles turning a brilliant gold.

Follow the trail for 0.6 mile to a junction with Trail 575 to Ferguson Lake (Hike 11). Veer left, staying on Trail 498 for a gentle descent along an open

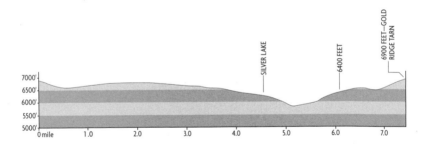

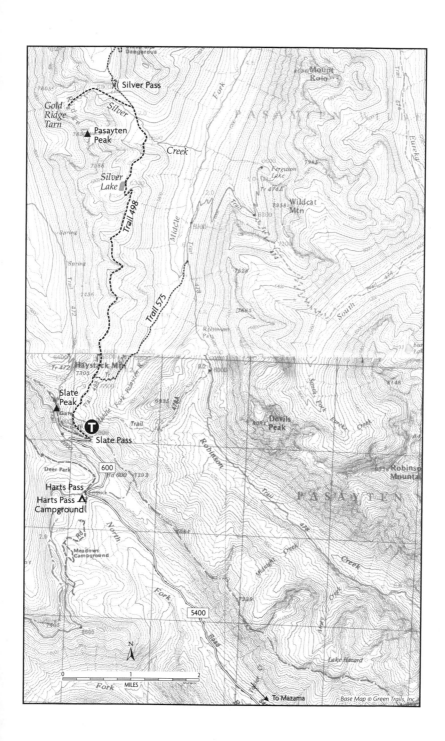

Buckskin Ridge is dotted with bright yellow alpine larches in October. (Photo by Alan L. Bauer)

hillside. Look behind you to see Silver Star in the distance, keep watch for wildlife, and remain alert amid some tricky footing near the talus rocks.

The trail covers 4.5 miles to Silver Lake, a good turnaround point for day hikers and a fine campsite for those uncomfortable with the idea of heading off trail toward Gold Ridge. The best campsites are about an eighth of a mile above the lake on the flat benches to the north, although pitching a tent here means every trip for water will require a walk up and down a steep hillside.

To reach Gold Ridge, follow the trail 1.5 miles north from Silver Lake. Beyond Silver Creek, at an elevation around 6400 feet, step off the trail to your left. (If you reach 6500-foot Silver Pass, hike back a bit. You have gone too far.) Angle up the hill toward the northwest. About 1.5 miles of steep and strenuous hiking will take you 1000 feet higher to the crest of Gold Ridge. The tarn (a fancy word meaning "mountain lake") sits northwest of 7850-foot Pasayten Peak and feeds the waters of Silver Creek.

Once at the tarn, tired hikers might believe they have arrived in heaven. Views above tree line are divine, and hikers' heads will spin as they take in this Okanogan panorama of craggy peaks and lofty ridges. Those who camp here overnight should rise early to explore the ridge and, if they are experienced climbers, scramble up Pasayten Peak—an airy experience not recommended for the fainthearted.

A final caution: Hikers should use extreme care once they return to the trailhead and begin driving home. At 6900 feet the steep road is sometimes coated in frost during September and October. Those who do not heed the weather reports before their trips may return to find their vehicles covered in snow.

11 FERGUSON LAKE

Distance	■	**14.6 miles (round trip)**
Hiking time	■	2 days
Starting elevation	■	6900 feet
Low point	■	5200 feet
High point	■	6900 feet
Hikable	■	August through early October
Maps	■	Green Trails 18 Pasayten Peak and 50 Washington Pass; USGS Pasayten Peak
Information	■	Methow Valley Visitor Center, Okanogan National Forest, 509-996-4000

Colonel W. Thomas Hart had money on his mind in 1900 when he pushed what would become the state's highest road through this rugged terrain. Hart was looking for an easy way to move gold out of Harts Pass into town. Today, hikers can follow Hart's trail up to see the rare jewel known as Ferguson Lake, an excellent overnight destination. The only problem is the dramatic dip this trail takes to cross the Middle Fork of the Pasayten River—a withering bit of elevation loss that will make hikers wish Hart had mined the riverbed instead of the peaks.

To reach the trailhead, follow State Route 20 to Mazama, 16 miles west of Winthrop. Follow Lost River Road (Forest Service Road 1183) to the northwest, and stay on it when it turns to gravel and becomes Forest Service Road (FS) 5400. Drive slowly and carefully along this narrow road for 20 miles beyond Mazama until you reach Harts Pass, site of some primitive car camp spots. From Harts Pass, go right on FS 600, drive another 1.5 miles, and park at a place identified on maps as Slate Pass, starting points for Trails 498 and 575. (To drive on the highest road in Washington state, go another mile to Slate Peak, location of a 7440-foot lookout.)

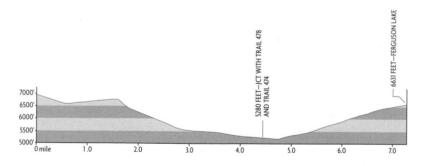

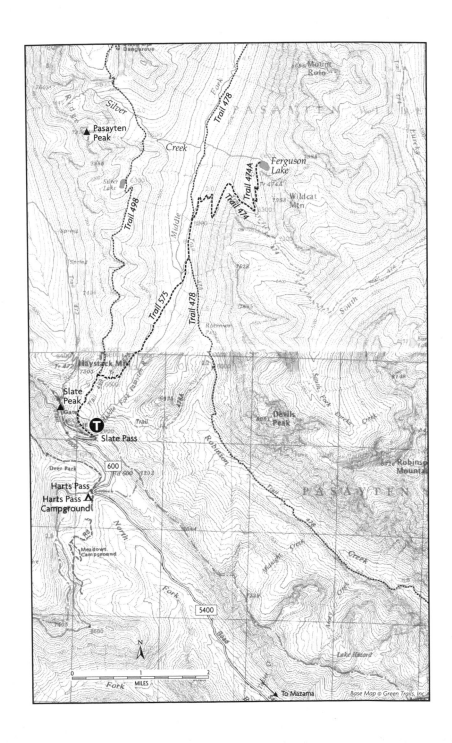

The trail starts from a scenic trailhead where larches turn a spectacular gold in late September or early October. The trail drops 0.6 mile to a junction with the trail heading to Silver Pass (described in Hike 10). Veer right onto Trail 575 toward the Middle Fork of the Pasayten River.

The trail descends from here, losing roughly 1700 feet from the trailhead elevation by the time hikers have covered 2.2 miles The trail bottoms out temporarily around 5200 feet as it crosses the river and then rises a bit on the far shore up to a 5280-foot junction with Trail 478.

Turn left at the junction and follow Trail 478 north alongside the Middle Fork. After 0.6 mile, turn right at a junction with Trail 474 and brace your muscles to regain the elevation just lost.

Trail 474 rises 1100 feet in 2 miles to a junction with Trail 474A. Turn left here and head north 1 mile to 6631-foot Ferguson Lake, an excellent spot to enjoy the scenery and perhaps wet a fishing line to catch your dinner. The best campsites lie north of the lake on flat benches about 200 feet above the shore. Views above tree line here reveal 8096-foot Mount Rolo to the north, 7958-foot Wildcat Mountain to the east, and the shoulder of 7850-foot Pasayten Peak to the west.

Options for side trips are unlimited in this portion of the 530,000-acre Pasayten Wilderness. Those with mountaineering experience can head north along the nearby ridge and scramble up Mount Rolo, and anglers who are not catching anything at Ferguson Lake can trace the ridge up to more isolated Freds Lake.

Return the way you came, but use caution once you reach the parking lot. Frost often coats the steep roads leading down from the trailhead.

The lush yellows of the alpine larch cover the Middle Fork Pasayten River Valley in October. (Photo by Alan L. Bauer)

12 PUGH RIDGE

Distance ■	**14.2 miles (round trip)**
Hiking time ■	7 to 8 hours, or 2 days
Starting elevation ■	3950 feet
High point ■	7000 feet
Hikable ■	Mid-July through September
Maps ■	Green Trails 114 Lucerne; USGS Pyramid Mountain
Information ■	Entiat Ranger District, Wenatchee National Forest, 509-784-1511 (ask about Trails 1477, 1438, 1439)

A spreading vista atop a bloom-choked ridge crest lies at the heart of this scenic loop. Along the way, hikers can sample shaded forest, open meadows, babbling brooks, and a few challenging river crossings—at least until the bridges are repaired. The clockwise route described here lets hikers travel uphill on the steepest section of the loop; this way they strain muscles rather than joints and can enjoy a long, leisurely downhill stroll once the hard work is out of the way. (If this is not to your liking, feel free to reverse course.)

From Wenatchee, head north to Entiat on Alternate US 97 (the highway on the west side of Lake Entiat, a lake's width away from US 97). Turn left onto Entiat River Road and drive 25 miles, at which point the road becomes Forest Service Road (FS) 51. Continue until the pavement ends just past Entiat Falls, then veer right at the Y onto FS 5606, following signs to the North Fork trailhead about 4 miles beyond at the end of the gravel road.

North Fork Trail 1437 dips briefly to cross Crow Creek then begins an undulating ascent through pine forest. Birdsong mixes with the constant rush of the North Fork of the Entiat River, which is close enough to be heard but too shaded to be seen.

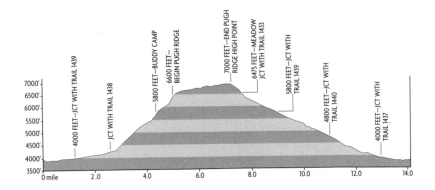

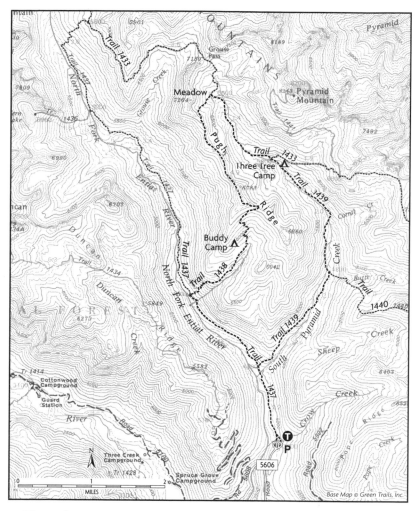

The trail crosses South Pyramid Creek in just over a mile and, soon after, hikers reach a junction with Trail 1439, the route they will take on their return. Another 1.5 miles of gentle stroll brings hikers to Pugh Ridge Trail 1438, where the real work begins.

The trail switchbacks steeply for its first mile, moderates a bit, then goes steep again. At 5800 feet, the trail passes the small lupine-filled meadow of "Buddy Camp," a good spot for a snack but a rather steep place to pitch a tent. A creek fed by melting snow babbles nearby.

More switchbacks lead to 6475 feet, where the dense evergreens thin out enough to allow some sunshine and give hikers their first views of the crags on the other side of the Entiat River. A final push leads to 6600 feet

Pyramid Mountain as seen from Pugh Ridge. (Photo by Skip Card)

and the flower-dotted crest of Pugh Ridge. Here hikers can gaze out at the cone-shaped profile of 8243-foot Pyramid Mountain and, farther north, the craggy head of 8590-foot Cardinal Mountain.

The trail grows vague in spots as it leads hikers up and along the ridge crest. As you take in the scenery, look for rock cairns designed to channel wanderers back to the true path. Camping is allowed on the dry ridge, but backpackers are urged to pitch tents atop old campsites and use existing fire rings.

The ridge trail rises, falls, and rises again until it tops out at 7000 feet. It then begins a steep and often slippery (snow lingers longest here) descent to a 6475-foot meadow near the headwaters of South Pyramid Creek and a junction with Pyramid Mountain Trail 1433. From the junction, Trail 1433 descends gently amid sunny meadows and well-spaced trees, rarely far from the creek's tumbling waters.

After 1.4 miles, veer right at the junction onto Pyramid Creek Trail 1439. The meadow near the junction offers the best views of Pugh Ridge, so take a moment to gaze up at what you just left. Stay on Trail 1439 for 4 miles back to the North Fork. The easy grade is interrupted only by one or two creek crossings that might require a wade until washed-out log bridges can be restored.

Once back on Trail 1437, turn left and retrace your earlier steps back to the parking lot.

Facing page: Fall is a great time to enjoy the colors of the Chiwawa River Valley. (Photo by Alan L. Bauer)

STEVENS PASS EAST RAIN SHADOW

The region stretching east from Stevens Pass begins amid glacier-coated peaks like Clark Mountain and ends in the dry summer trails around Leavenworth. The change is clearly visible. Areas on the west slopes of Stevens Pass might receive 160 inches of rain a year, largely because of moisture channeled by the Puget Sound Convergence Zone. Meanwhile, Leavenworth averages 25.3 inches of annual rainfall, and less than an inch of rain typically falls in the area during the driest summer months.

Yet, rain gauges are only one way to spot a rain shadow. Trees are another indicator. Lodgepole and ponderosa pines often grow on the dry hillsides east of Stevens Pass, while the wet areas to the west yield the giant moisture-loving Douglas fir. Ground cover changes, too. As rainfall decreases, common shrubs like salal and fern are replaced by kinnickinnick and more abundant displays of lupine, paintbrush, and other wildflowers.

Dry climates have dangers, too. Wildfires can start quickly in arid regions when lightning strikes dry forest without any accompanying rain. Many trails on the east slopes of the Cascades—including Windy Pass and Alpine Lookout—pass near hillsides that were blackened by forest fires. In 1970 alone, more than 400 separate fires burned 122,000 acres in the Wenatchee National Forest.

It is often not dangerous hiking in fire-prone areas, largely because rangers and other officials are quick to close lands threatened by fire. Still, hikers and backpackers can reduce their risk by calling or stopping by local ranger stations to get the latest updates on fire activity. They also can dramatically reduce the threat of fire by making sure any campfires remain small and under control—and most of all by completely drowning their fires, stirring the ashes, and feeling the soaked coals to make sure no hot embers will linger after they leave. When conditions are dangerously dry, it is critical that everyone respect all bans on outdoor burning.

Areas that have been scorched by fire often remain closed for several years so hikers will not be struck by charred trees that can easily topple during windstorms. Such closures also allow the ecosystems to recover, as seasonal fires are a normal part of the natural cycle in some dry regions. To germinate and sprout, lodgepole pine's seeds require the heat generated by fire, and Thompson's clover with its big purple blossoms grows back more thickly after a wildfire. Hikers who revisit hillsides that were scarred by fire are often surprised by the forest's resiliency and its steady recovery.

The trails in this section all get about the same amount of annual rainfall, but the hikes outside Leavenworth deserve special mention. Hikers who drive to the far end of Leavenworth's Icicle Road will have headed west for 15 miles. The end of the road puts them just 7 miles east of the Cascades crest—close enough to lose some of the rain shadow's sheltering effects. (If you get rained on, head east next time.)

13 BASALT PASS

Distance	■	**5.8 miles (round trip, longer with view detours)**
Hiking time	■	4 to 6 hours
Starting elevation	■	3700 feet
High point	■	6004 feet
Hikable	■	Late June through October
Maps	■	Green Trails 146 Plain and 114 Lucerne; USGS Schafer Lake
Information	■	Lake Wenatchee Ranger District, Wenatchee National Forest, 509-763-3103

The western edge of the rugged Entiat Mountains lets hikers sample sights and scents from both sides of the Cascades. Trails in the region often wind among the towering Douglas fir and lush green ground cover found primarily in the western Cascades, yet hikers also see the ponderosa pine typical of the eastern Cascades. The region gets less than half the rainfall of Stevens Pass, yet streams and lakes are plentiful. Such characteristics, combined with stunning views from lofty viewpoints, make little-known Basalt Pass a worthwhile excursion.

To reach the Basalt Pass trailhead, drive east of Stevens Pass on US 2 and turn north at Coles Corner onto State Route 207. Follow the highway toward Lake Wenatchee for 4.3 miles and, after crossing the Wenatchee River, turn right at the Y onto County Road 22 (also known as Chiwawa Loop Road). Drive 1.3 miles and turn left onto Chiwawa Valley Road (which will in turn become Forest Service Road (FS) 62, and ultimately FS 6200). Drive 9.5 miles and turn right on FS 6210. Drive 5.8 miles, past two trailheads, to Basalt Pass Trail 1530. Trailhead elevation is roughly 3700 feet. Parking is limited.

The trail heads steeply uphill, with only occasional level patches, as it follows alongside a stream that trickles into Chikamin Creek. Two stream crossings appear quickly, but these are often dry by fall and challenging only during the height of the spring melt. Hikers catch glimpses of tree-covered Basalt

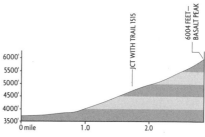

Peak as they pass through a canopy of towering silver fir. The understory is dotted with golden-yellow Douglas maple, vanilla leaf, and Solomon seal—plants that fade beautifully each colorful fall.

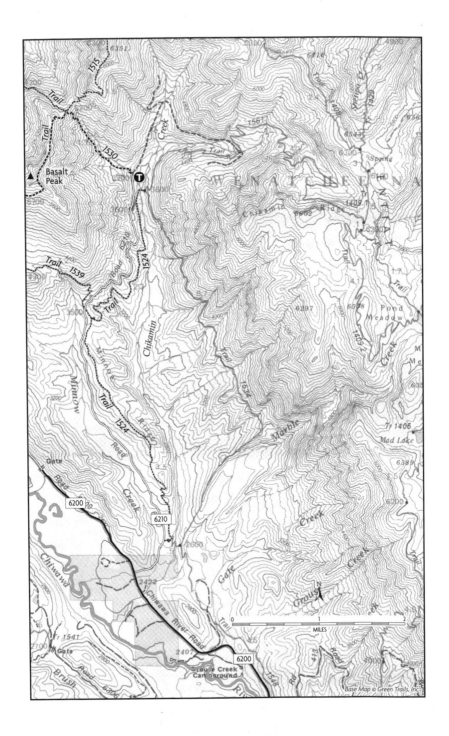

After 1.7 miles, turn left at the junction with Trail 1515 to head south 1.2 miles to 6004-foot Basalt Peak. Many hikers stop here, content with climbing about 2300 feet in 2.9 miles.

Anyone with some gas left in the tank after bagging Basalt should head back to the trail junction and continue east on Trail 1515. The primitive ridge trail heads deep into the Entiat Mountains, toward 7535-foot Garland Peak,

The view of the Chiwawa River Valley from Basalt Ridge is lonely and beautiful. (Photo by Alan L. Bauer)

but hikers only have to go a short distance up the trail for rewarding views. Excellent viewpoints appear after 1 mile, around 5700 feet, and again after 2 miles, where hikers skirt an open northwest slope below a 6754-foot peak. The views consist of Basalt Peak, of course, but hikers also can look south to see Icicle Ridge and part of Mount Stuart. To the west across the Chiwawa River Valley stands 7420-foot Mount David.

Basalt Pass is especially scenic in fall, when its broad hillside fills with the yellows of Douglas maples, the oranges from Sitka mountain ash, and the crimson from huckleberries. Distant hillsides and valleys turn golden from the fading larch trees.

14 ALPINE LOOKOUT

Distance ■	5.2 miles to lookout (one way); 11.6 miles to Merritt Lake Trailhead (one way)
Hiking time ■	3 hours to lookout; 5 hours to Merritt Lake Trailhead
Starting elevation ■	3900 feet
High point ■	6237 feet
Hikable ■	Late June through mid-October
Maps ■	Green Trails 145 Wenatchee Lake; USGS Lake Wenatchee
Information ■	Lake Wenatchee Ranger District, Wenatchee National Forest, 509-763-3103

High ridge walking, stunning vistas in all directions, and close proximity to the Puget Sound region all help explain why Alpine Lookout is one of the classic hikes in the Cascades. It is also relatively simple to turn the trip

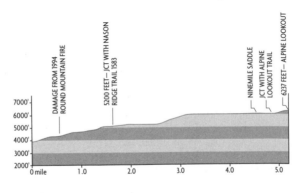

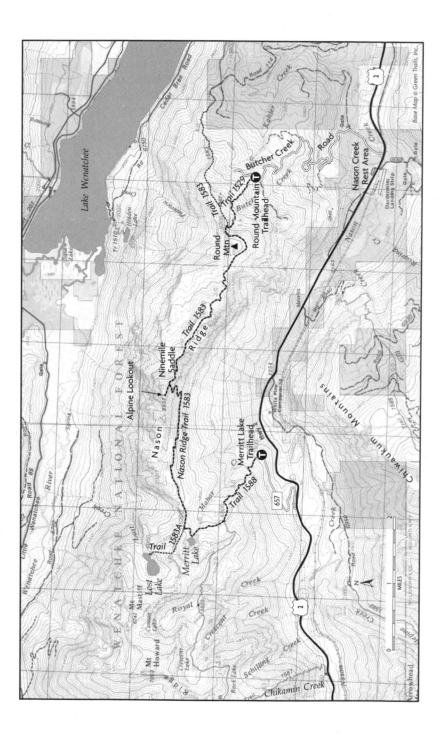

Base Map © Green Trails, Inc.

into an exhilarating one-way trek, with the use of a second vehicle. Situated between very wet and very dry zones, the Alpine Lookout route will usually be dry even when nearby Stevens Pass gets drizzling rain from a marine push. The trail also offers the opportunity to study Mother Nature's successful efforts to restore the land following the devastating fires of 1994. With some patience, you might also spot the mountain goat herd that makes its home near this high ridge.

To reach the trailhead, travel on US 2 to the junction with Butcher Creek Road just east of the Nason Creek Rest Area on the north side of the highway near milepost 82. Proceed up Butcher Creek Road about 3 miles, avoiding all side roads and being wary of possible logging traffic. Hikers planning a one-way trip should leave a second vehicle at the Merritt Lake trailhead. To get there, turn north off US 2 near milepost 77 at the spur road to Merritt Lake, and drive 1.5 miles up Forest Service Road 657.

Trail 1529 begins immediately at a rather steep angle, and within 0.5 mile hikers enter an area heavily damaged by the Round Mountain fire of 1994. Hikers cannot help but notice the dramatic contrast between the rich green colors of nature's new growth and the milky white bark of the burned trees. Continue climbing steeply through this burned area for a little over a mile, before leveling out just before the 5200-foot junction with Nason Ridge Trail 1583. Turn left, and soon reach a dramatic overlook above Lake Wenatchee.

For the next 3 miles, the trail meanders from one side of Nason Ridge to the other, gradually gaining elevation. Views become increasingly rewarding, whether it be the rugged Chiwaukum Mountains to the south or the spectacular topography of the Glacier Peak region to the north. Just past 4.6 miles from the trailhead, drop through a dramatic rocky area known as Ninemile Saddle, and from there proceed 0.3 mile west up to the junction with the Alpine Lookout Trail. Turn right and climb a short 0.3 mile to the lookout, while keeping alert for mountain goats on the rocky crags just below the ridge. Alpine Lookout sits at 6237 feet.

Lightning storms are a common cause of forest fires in the eastern Cascades, and the commanding views from the peak make Alpine Lookout well situated for early detection. The site was established as a fire watch in 1920, the first permanent building was constructed in 1936, and the current structure was built in 1975. The lookout is still staffed by Wenatchee National Forest personnel during the fire season, which generally runs from mid-July through late September. Alpine Lookout is listed on the official National Historic Lookout Register.

Hikers can descend the way they came, for a total distance of 10.4 miles.

Those making a one-way trip to the Merritt Lake trailhead should return to the junction with the Nason Ridge Trail and turn right onto Trail 1583. The trail begins with a series of steep switchbacks down a broad hillside of large

Facing page: View to the west from just below Alpine Lookout.
(Photo by Don Hanson)

boulders, but eventually the path levels out around 5200 feet. Continue west for 3.1 miles to the junction with an unmarked trailhead. Proceed south, down past the shore of Merritt Lake, for 1 mile to the junction with Trail 1588. Follow Trail 1588 for 2 miles down to the parking lot.

15 LAKE JULIUS, LOCH EILEEN, AND LAKE DONALD

Distance ■	14.2 miles to Loch Eileen (one way)
Hiking time ■	3 to 4 days
Starting elevation ■	2200 feet
High point ■	5870 feet
Hikable ■	August through mid-October
Maps ■	Green Trails 177 Chiwaukum Mountains; USGS Chiwaukum Lake
Information ■	Leavenworth Ranger District, Wenatchee National Forest, 509-548-6977 (ask about trails to Loch Eileen and Lake Julius)

This scenic trail takes hikers past four pristine lakes with wonderful views and limited crowds. The catch? You will have to backpack. When you do, time your trip to miss the thick swarms of insects usually present in July and August. Wise hikers often visit after Labor Day, when the first freeze has tamed the 'skeeters and the larch needles begin to turn golden.

From US 2, go 0.75 mile west of Tumwater Creek Campground (8.7 miles west of Leavenworth) and turn onto Chiwaukum Creek Road (Forest Service Road 7908). Drive 0.25 mile to the point where the road is blocked.

The route along Chiwaukum Creek starts with 1.25 miles of walkable road before hikers reach the trailhead and the true beginning of Trail 1571. The trail meanders along Chiwaukum Creek, slowly gaining elevation.

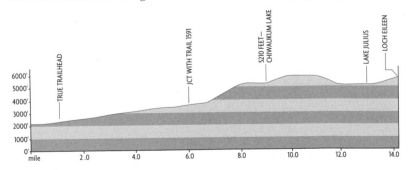

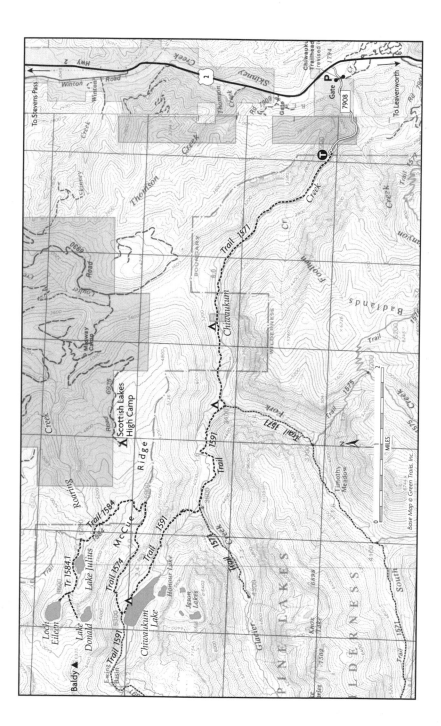

Hikers enjoy the beauty of pristine Lake Donald. (Photo by Don Hanson)

Good campsites will appear at Chiwaukum Lake, 9.2 miles from the parking lot, but backpackers who find that distance daunting can choose a site elsewhere along the creek.

Trail 1571 covers 5.2 miles until it reaches a junction with Trail 1591 near the creek's south fork. Veer right onto Trail 1591 and continue west. Good alternative campsites appear in about a mile, and in another 0.6 mile the trail passes a junction with Trail 1573. Stay right and continue on 1591.

From here, the trail rises about 1400 feet in 2.4 miles on its way up to 5210-foot Chiwaukum Lake. Good views await hikers once they reach the lake. Better views lie even farther ahead.

Near the north end of Chiwaukum Lake, find Trail 1574 and follow it up and east for 2 miles, to where it joins Trail 1584. Turn left and follow 1584 north for 1.5 miles to the junction with Trail 1584.1 to Lake Julius. Turn left and head west toward the lake's outlet about 0.3 mile away. There are some campsites near the lake. Hikers can also go to Loch Eileen, located 1.2 miles from the junction. When you reach the lake, notice the grove of larch trees just south of the lake's outlet; in October, these deciduous conifers turn brilliant gold before shedding their needles. Hikers who make it to Loch Eileen will have covered 14.2 miles and risen 3670 feet from the trailhead—not counting all the minor ups and downs. There are camping areas here.

To reach Lake Donald, cross Loch Eileen's outlet and head southwest along a faint 0.5-mile uphill path marked by rock cairns. The trail to this lake is a fisherman's trail. Since Lake Donald is a pristine environment, hikers need to practice "Leave No Trace" techniques to minimize their impact. No camping is allowed. High meadows beckon everywhere around Lake Donald, and views are sublime. An easy walk leads up to the summit of Baldy, the local name for the prominent high point north of the lake.

From here, hikers can see Nason Ridge, countless peaks, and, far below, the ribbon of asphalt that identifies US 2. Hikers who turn south of Lake Donald and scramble 1 mile up McCue Ridge to Tamarack Point will see an excellent view of Larch Lake (Hike 16).

Hikers who do not want to backpack can reach Lake Donald after a 3.5-mile hike from Scottish Lakes High Camp, a private resort. For details, call 425-844-2000, or visit the website at *www.scottishlakes.com*.

16 LARCH LAKE

Distance ■	**22.8 miles (round trip)**
Hiking time ■	2–3 days
Starting elevation ■	2200 feet
High point ■	6100 feet
Hikable ■	Mid-July through mid-October
Maps ■	Green Trails 177 Chiwaukum Mountains; USGS Chiwaukum Lake
Information ■	Leavenworth Ranger District, Wenatchee National Forest, 509-548-6977 (ask about trails to Larch Lake)

Some consider this trail into the Alpine Lakes Wilderness to be one of the greatest hikes in the Northwest—but timing is important. Arrive in midsummer, and the bugs will eat you alive. Wait too long, and you might get coated with snow. The ideal weather window runs from September until

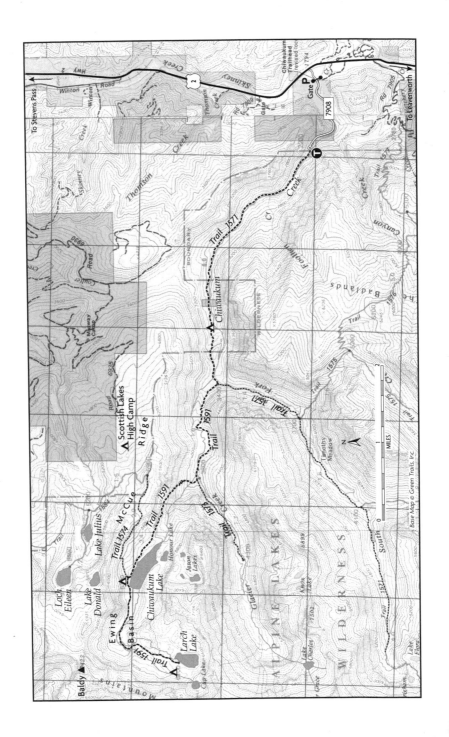

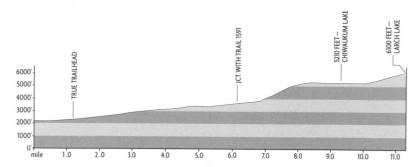

early October: peak time to see the golden larches that surround the lake.

From US 2, go 0.75 mile west of Tumwater Creek Campground (8.7 miles west of Leavenworth) and turn onto Chiwaukum Creek Road (Forest Service Road 7908). Drive 0.25 mile to the point where the road is blocked.

The route along Chiwaukum Creek starts with 1.25 miles of walkable road before hikers reach the trailhead and the true beginning of Trail 1571. The trail meanders along Chiwaukum Creek, slowly gaining elevation. Good campsites can be found 3 or 4 miles in. After 5.2 miles, the trail reaches a junction with Trail 1591 near the creek's south fork. Veer right onto 1591 and continue west. In another 1.6 miles, the trail passes a junction with Trail 1573. Stay right and continue on 1591.

The shores of Larch Lake are blazed in gold in autumn.
(Photo by Michael Fagin)

From here, the trail becomes a grind, rising about 1400 feet in 2.4 miles on its way up to 5210-foot Chiwaukum Lake. Enjoy a lunch break here, or maybe even a swim.

Larch Lake sits 2.2 miles beyond Chiwaukum Lake along a scenic path that displays dramatic color every autumn. The fall foliage is awesome among the trees in Ewing Basin, but even the trailside rocks tend to turn red as ground cover shifts with the season.

When you reach Larch Lake, lie back along the shore and let the world go by. Imagine how lovely it would be to stay in such a wonderland—so long as winter never arrived, snow never fell, and bugs did not exist. When the dreaming is done, set up camp, cook dinner, and plan the next day's cross-country field trips. For trip suggestions, just look at the map and select among the area's numerous lakes.

Hikers seeking a shorter journey can reach Larch Lake after a 6-mile trek from Scottish Lakes High Camp, a private resort. For details, call 425-844-2000, or visit the website at *www.scottishlakes.com.*

17 WINDY PASS

Distance ■	**15.6 miles (round trip)**
Hiking time ■	8 to 10 hours
Starting elevation ■	3300 feet
High point ■	7200 feet
Hikable ■	Mid-July through October
Maps ■	Green Trails 177 Chiwaukum Mountains; USGS Chiwaukum Mountains
Information ■	Leavenworth Ranger District, Wenatchee National Forest, 509-548-6977 (ask about Eightmile Creek Trail 1552 and Trail 1554 to Windy Pass)

Many old-timers can remember back to 1993 when backpackers could drop their packs and tent at Lake Caroline without first getting an overnight permit. Those days are gone, but this area is still worth a visit. Besides, the areas around Eightmile Lake and Lake Caroline are not as popular as the Enchantments, and overnight permits are easier to obtain. Even if all the permits are snapped up, day hikers who get an early start can still trek in to Lake Caroline (9.6 miles round trip round trip) or go all the way to the scenic splendor of Windy Pass (15.6 miles round trip), and then return to Leavenworth for a cold beer, some bratwurst, and a hotel.

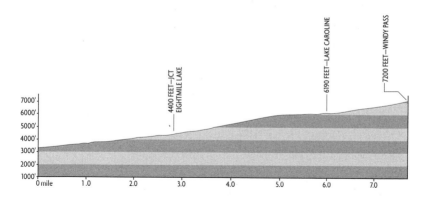

From Leavenworth, turn south off US 2 onto Icicle Creek Road, which morphs into Forest Service Road (FS) 76. Follow this road for 8.3 miles, then turn left onto Eightmile Creek Road (FS 7601). Cross the bridge and go 3 steep miles to the trailhead parking lot. On-site wilderness registration is required, permits are needed for overnight camping, and no dogs—not even dogs on leashes—are allowed on the trail.

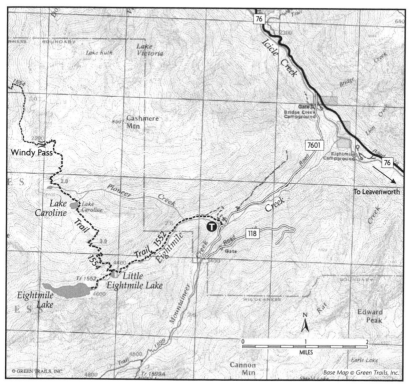

Lake Caroline is the main attraction along the way to Windy Pass.
(Photo by Alan L. Bauer)

Trail 1552 usually begins beneath sunny skies typical of the eastern Cascades, and flowers bloom alongside the trail in early summer. After 2.8 miles of steady but rarely steep elevation gain, hikers reach Little Eightmile Lake and a junction with Trail 1554 to Lake Caroline and Windy Pass. Many day hikers continue another 0.5 mile to 4641-foot Eightmile Lake, a good early-season destination since the trail often melts out by late May. By June, the lake is a worthy overnight campsite for hikers who want to split their Windy Pass trip over two days.

From the junction, Trail 1554 climbs steeply up a hillside that was severely scarred by fire in 1994. Hikers can marvel at the forest's resiliency as they switchback up the trail amid an abundance of wildflowers springing from the charred wood and ash. Views of the Stuart Range open up as the climb continues.

Scenic Lake Caroline appears 5.8 miles from the trailhead, tucked away among the pines and rocks at 6190 feet elevation. Few will feel cheated if they choose this as their turnaround point, but even better views await 2 miles ahead.

Pushing on toward Windy Pass, hikers soon pass Little Lake Caroline tucked away in a small meadow. The trail steepens beyond the small lake, rising more than 1000 feet in the final 1.5 miles. Sweaty hikers who arrive during the peak bloom from mid-July to early August can witness a vast flower show that springs up about a mile below the pass.

If the flowers are not on display, head upward toward the views at the 7200-foot pass, which seems to reveal the entire sweep of the central Cascades. Sloan Peak, Mount Daniel, and the Stuart Range highlight this peak show, but numerous other crags are visible.

Serious mountaineers use Windy Pass as their access to 8501-foot Cashmere Mountain. Casual hikers might sample the approach march, but the climb itself should be attempted only by experienced climbers.

18 COLCHUCK LAKE

Distance ■	**8.2 miles (round trip)**
Hiking time ■	8.5 hours
Starting elevation ■	3400 feet
High point ■	5600 feet
Hikable ■	Mid-July to October
Maps ■	Green Trails 209 Mount Stuart and 177 Chiwaukum Mountains; USGS Chiwaukum Mountains and Mount Stuart
Information ■	Leavenworth Ranger District, Wenatchee National Forest, 509-548-6977

A day in Paradise? Not exactly. An enchanting evening? Almost. The trail to Colchuck Lake will get you right to the edge of the famous Enchantments, and the lake's deep green water and glacier-polished rocks offer much of the beauty available farther down the tightly regulated trail. Best of all, day hikers do not need a permit to sample the scenery.

From Leavenworth, turn south off US 2 onto Icicle Creek Road, which morphs into Forest Service Road (FS) 76. Follow this road for 8.3 miles, then turn left onto Eightmile Creek Road (FS 7601). Cross the bridge and go 4 steep miles to the trailhead parking lot near the end of the road. On-site

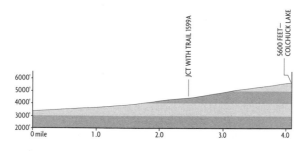

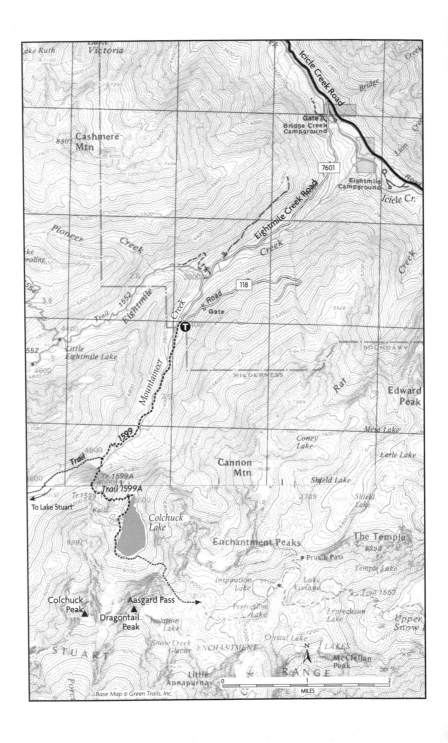

wilderness registration is required. Overnight backpackers must obtain permits (supply limited) at the Leavenworth Ranger Station.

As if to preserve its views for the finale, Trail 1599 starts off in mundane fashion beneath the heavy cover of shady forest. Following alongside Mountaineer Creek, the trail rises gently to gain 1100 feet in 2.5 miles until a junction with Trail 1599A. Avoid the right turn to Lake Stuart and go left onto 1599A, a steep path that will take hikers 1100 vertical feet in 1.6 miles. Elevation gain ends at the green waters of Colchuck Lake.

Backpackers who have received the coveted overnight permits use this trail as a jumping-off point for their trips into the Enchantments, the string of starkly beautiful but extremely fragile (and therefore tightly restricted) lakes that lie north of the Stuart Range. Climbers also pass Colchuck Lake on their way to climb Dragontail Peak and Colchuck Peak.

For day hikers, Colchuck Lake is a worthy destination. Walk south along the length of the lakeshore, following the trail for a mile, to drink in the lake's alpine loveliness. If time allows, go a little farther, following the trail as it curls east and gains elevation to reveal unforgettable views of Colchuck and Dragontail Peaks.

Hikers who continue on this trail will reach 7800-foot Aasgard Pass, the gateway into the Enchantments. Casual hikers should turn back well before this point. This unmaintained trail is steep and littered with loose rocks—a challenge for anyone carrying a pack.

View of Colchuck Lake seen along the hike toward Aasgard Pass.
(Photo by Michael Fagin)

19 JACK CREEK TO MEADOW CREEK

Distance ■	**13.4 miles (round trip)**
Hiking time ■	5 to 6 hours
Starting elevation ■	2840 feet
High point ■	4080 feet
Hikable ■	Mid-July through early October
Maps ■	Green Trails 177 Chiwaukum Mountains; USGS Jack Ridge
Information ■	Leavenworth Ranger District, Wenatchee National Forest, 509-548-6977 (ask about Jack Creek Trail 1558 and Meadow Creek Trail 1559)

Solitude and level paths are in short supply near Leavenworth's popular Icicle Creek, the river that divides rugged Icicle Ridge from the steep peaks in the northern Alpine Lakes region. Still, a lonely and mostly level trail can be found along Jack Creek, and hikers prepared to ford streams and cover some distance can reach one of the most scenic meadows in the state.

From Leavenworth, turn south off US 2 onto Icicle Creek Road. Follow the road (which becomes Forest Service Road (FS) 76 and, when the pavement ends, FS 7600) for 17 miles. Veer left near Rock Island Campground, cross the bridge over Icicle Creek, and, just beyond the bridge, turn left onto FS 615. Drive 0.1 mile and turn right into the trailhead parking lot.

Trail 1558 begins in sun but ascends into stands of hemlock and pine shortly after hikers cross the stout bridge over Jack Creek. Experienced hikers linger a bit beyond the bridge on the exposed hillsides, which offer some of the best creekside views of the entire trek.

The trail climbs steadily through the well-spaced trees for 1.2 miles until it reaches a junction with Trout Creek Trail 1555, a popular turnoff that often helps thin the crowds. Stay on 1558. The path is more level for the next 1.8

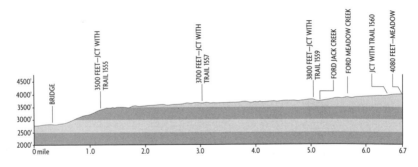

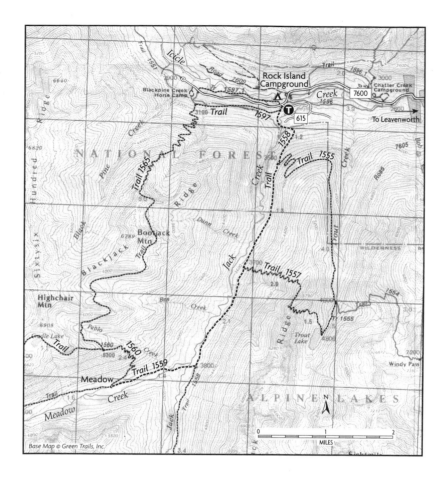

Base Map © Green Trails, Inc.

miles until the junction with Trail 1557, a steep path that descends directly down from Trout Lake to complete a popular loop. The junction is a popular rest stop with good views of Jack Creek, which is rarely seen during these initial miles although its tumbling rapids are constantly heard.

The next 2.1 miles of Trail 1558 trace a mostly level path through sometimes marshy ground where green foliage often grows thick enough to crowd the trail. A few water-loving wildflowers can be spotted here, chiefly the low-growing bunchberry (also known as Canadian dogwood) with its four white bracts set amid veined green leaves.

A junction with Meadow Creek Trail 1559 appears 5.1 miles from the trailhead. Turn right, walk a few hundred yards and then figure out how you are going to get across Jack Creek. The creek pools enough here that hikers who remembered to carry sandals and trekking poles should have little trouble wading to the far side. Others should head downstream a

Harding Mountain rises above the meadow of Meadow Creek.
(Photo by Skip Card)

bit to scout a dry crossing over bridges formed by fallen logs—a tricky endeavor not recommended for children or anyone lacking sure feet.

Once across Jack Creek, hikers go 0.5 mile before they must ford Meadow Creek—a tricky crossing in the same way Jack Creek is, although Meadow is appreciably smaller. After another mile through the woods, just past the junction with Snowall–Cradle Lake Trail 1560, the thick woods open to a broad meadow on a gently sloping hillside.

Even jaded hikers might find themselves awestruck by the sight of this tree-fringed oasis. The 4080-foot meadow grows thick with blue lupine, orange tiger lilies, magenta paintbrush, and a variety of other colorful blooms. Framing all this scenery are rugged mountains, notably 7173-foot Harding Mountain hard to the south and the orange-brown crags of the Wenatchee Mountains farther to the west.

Pull up a boulder, rest your wet feet, and drink it all in—alone, if you are lucky.

SALMON LA SAC
RAIN SHADOW

n the 1890s, prospectors headed to places like Salmon la Sac, Roslyn, and Cle Elum in search of gold, silver, iron, and coal. Today, people flock to these areas to escape the rain of the western Cascades.

Numbers do not lie. Snoqualmie Pass in the teeth of the moisture zone gets 104.7 inches of rain in a typical year. Travel 10 miles east, and Lake Kachess receives just 53.5 inches. The skies dry out the farther east you go: Cle Elum Lake 8 miles beyond Lake Kachess gets 37.2 inches of rain. By the time clouds reach Cle Elum another 8 miles east, the rain shadow effect has squeezed out so much moisture that yearly rainfall is down to 22.3 inches. Put 26 miles behind you, and you've lost more than 82 inches of annual rainfall.

Still, Salmon la Sac is far enough to the west that weather experts consider it merely a partial rain shadow. Expect a few more clouds here than you would in more easterly areas like Cle Elum—and since most people pass close to Cle Elum as they drive to Salmon la Sac, do not be surprised if a few clouds gather as you motor west to the trailhead. Still, hikers should find far drier weather conditions (and a few less crowds) here than they would on the trails near Snoqualmie Pass. In most cases, areas west of Cle Elum get 40 percent of the rain seen in the pass.

The wettest hikes in this fairly dry area are the ones closest to 7899-foot Mount Daniel, the area's tallest peak. Set a little east of the Cascades crest, and technically in King County, Daniel still gets roughly 140 to 160 inches of rain a year and has several active glaciers—shrinking, to be sure, but nevertheless active.

Consider these factors as you choose your hikes. Peggy's Pond at the doorstep of Mount Daniel will get some rain shadow benefits. Hikers who want a drier environment should choose more easterly hikes such as Davis Peak.

Preceding page: The Silver Creek Trail along Kachess Ridge passes directly under this massive rocky peak. (Photo by Alan L. Bauer)

20 | POLALLIE RIDGE TO DIAMOND LAKE

Distance	▪	**8.8 miles (round trip)**
Hiking time	▪	4 to 5 hours
Starting elevation	▪	2510 feet
High point	▪	5144 feet
Hikable	▪	Mid-July through September
Maps	▪	Green Trails 208 Kachess Lake; USGS Polallie Ridge, Davis Peak
Information	▪	Cle Elum Ranger District, Wenatchee National Forest, 509-674-4411 (ask about Polallie Ridge Trail 1309)

Alpine views, shaded forests, and some sun-dappled meadows highlight the path along Polallie Ridge to lovely Diamond Lake. Elevation gain is steady, but fit hikers might find they have reached the lake before even working up a good sweat.

From Interstate 90, take exit 80 for Roslyn and Salmon la Sac and follow Bullfrog Road for 2.8 miles to the junction with State Route (SR) 903. Turn left onto SR 903 (sometimes called Salmon la Sac Road) and drive 16.5 miles, following signs to Salmon la Sac Campground. When the pavement ends, follow the main road across the bridge and, near the campground entrance, turn right, following signs to the Salmon la Sac trailheads. Drive 0.6 mile and park in the large lot near the Cooper River.

Three trails sprout quickly from this popular trailhead. Hikers following Polallie Ridge Trail 1309 should go right after 0.1 mile at the junction with Cooper River Trail 1311, and then veer left a few hundred feet later at the junction with Trail 1310 to Waptus Lake. (*Hikers beware:* Recent changes to the road and trails are not shown on the 1997 Green Trails map.)

Trail 1309 makes steady and sometimes steep uphill progress through pleasant pine forests along a dry path coated with gray dust, brown

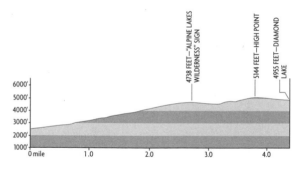

needles, and, in places, green horse poop. Step wisely. Views are spotty along the tree-coated ridge, although hikers are occasionally rewarded with an open meadow or sun-coated hillside.

About 2.6 miles in, land managers have erected an "Alpine Lakes Wilderness" sign to remind hikers of the boundary they have been tracing for most of their trip. The sign seems to work a bit of scenic magic, for here views open to reveal the rugged profile of 5295-foot Cone Mountain to the north.

The trail dips a bit beyond here, leading optimistic hikers to believe they are descending to Diamond Lake even though they are still almost 1.6 miles away. The trail soon rises again, dips briefly, rises one final time (to the trail's high point at 5144 feet), and finally descends the home stretch to the scenic lakeshore. Hikers might find the final miles a bit wet in early summer, as lingering snow's meltwater often flows in rivers down the

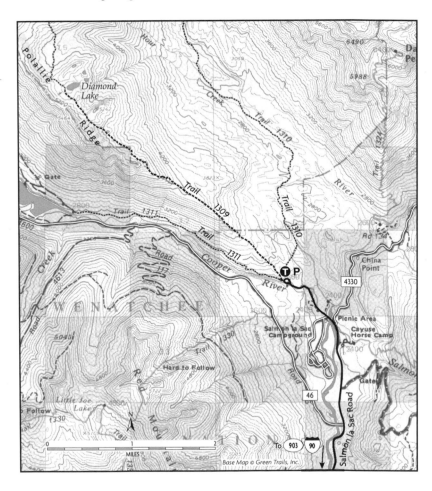

The Polallie Ridge Trail passes through several lush green meadows.
(Photo by Alan L. Bauer)

trail's rutted path. (When pathways are heavily snowed in, look for helpful blazes on trailside trees.)

Diamond Lake, elevation 4955 feet, provides an excellent spot to pull up a dead log, drink some water, swallow a candy bar, and (if your timing is bad) swat a million mosquitoes. Still, some spots are worth the DEET.

21 KACHESS RIDGE TO WEST PEAK

Distance ▪	**11 miles (round trip)**
Hiking time ▪	5 hours
Starting elevation ▪	2375 feet
High point ▪	5300 feet
Hikable ▪	July through September
Maps ▪	Green Trails 208 Kachess Lake; USGS Kachess Lake
Information ▪	Cle Elum Ranger District, Wenatchee National Forest, 509-674-4411 (ask about Trails 1315 and 1308.1)

The forests and small meadows on the trail below Kachess Ridge would please most hikers, but a seldom-used side route up to an eye-popping view of Mount Rainier gives this trek bonus scenery points. Start early to avoid getting sun-scorched on exposed hillsides, and pack some sandals (or at least a towel) in case Silver Creek has once again jumped its banks.

From Interstate 90, take exit 70 at Easton, head north, and turn left onto West Spark Road, following signs to Kachess Dam Road and Forest Service

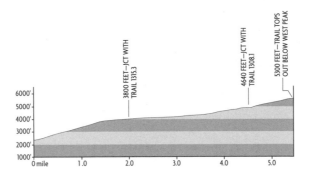

Roads (FS) 4818 through 4828. Drive 0.5 mile and turn right at the sign for Kachess Dam Road (also known as FS 4818). Follow the gravel for 0.8 mile, then turn right at the signs pointing to Trails 1315 and 1212. Drive 0.6 mile to the combined trailhead, and park where you can find room on the road's small shoulder.

Kachess Ridge Trail 1315 starts with a steep ascent along an often rocky and usually dusty series of fir-shaded switchbacks. Hikers might have to step aside to make room for horseback riders and bicyclists on this multi-use trail, although it is hard to imagine many bikers with enough muscle to pedal up the path's grueling first 0.5 mile.

After 1.3 miles, the path swings close to Silver Creek, a log-choked stream that will be a sidelong companion for much of the journey. The creek is respectful at this initial meeting, politely sticking to its streambed below the hillside trail.

At 1.9 miles, hikers pass a junction with Trail 1315.3, a 0.9-mile uphill side trail that leads to the top of a 4615-foot peak crowned by the Kachess Beacon Tower. Hikers with extra time can explore this detour, home to a relic of bygone days when beacons on this and other hilltops guided westbound pilots past Snoqualmie Pass peaks to Sea-Tac Airport.

A little beyond the junction, Silver Creek gets uppity and hikers reach the first of several spots where wading across the creek is often unavoidable. The problem is most severe when the creek swells with snowmelt, but sandals and trekking poles can come in handy at any time during unpredictable springs and summers.

The trail presses steadily (but rarely steeply) on its uphill path, crossing Silver Creek on occasion as it threads through forest interrupted by an occasional patch of meadow. About 4.3 miles from the trailhead, around 4550 feet elevation, the trails steps out of the thick trees toward a narrow and somewhat boggy clearing fringed with stunted subalpine firs. Here, hikers get their first glimpse of their destination, French Cabin Mountain's West Peak.

Look to the right as you walk the meadow path and spot the (typically) unmarked junction with Trail 1308.1. The narrow path heads eastward, crossing Silver Creek (a modest trickle here) before ascending steeply up the thinly wooded south-facing hillside toward the peak. Views improve with each uphill step during 1 mile of sunny switchbacks that put hikers at 5300 feet and a viewpoint just below West Peak's rocky nose.

Many peaks are visible here, but the star attraction is Mount Rainier and its rugged northeast face. Hikers gaze directly at Steamboat Prow, a triangular outcrop that splits Rainier's massive Emmons and Winthrop Glaciers. A little to the west is the fierce Willis Wall with the Carbon Glacier at its base.

Hikers with sure feet and nimble fingers can scramble higher up West Peak, gaining slightly better views as they near its 5724-foot summit.

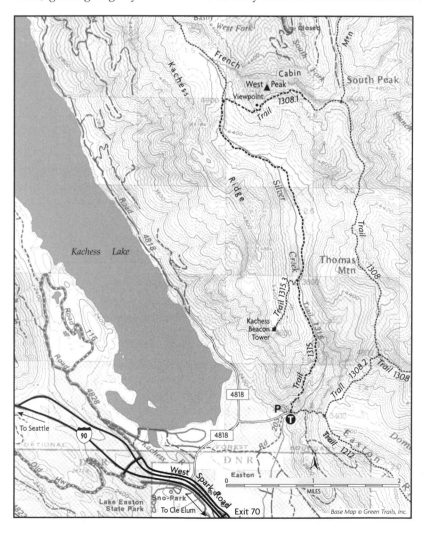

French Cabin Mountain's horseshoe-shaped ridge. (Photo by Skip Card)

People with expert routefinding skills can attempt to trace Trail 1308.1 another 1.6 miles as it traverses east to join Trail 1308. (Hikers successful at scouting this unmaintained and often snowed-covered path can then follow Trail 1308 south for 3.5 miles and a junction with a connector trail that leads back to the original trailhead—a 12.8-mile loop.)

Most hikers merely stop at 5300 feet, tiptoe through the lupine a short distance up the rock-strewn slope, and sit to eat some granola and drink in the views. Return the way you came, but as you are repacking for the descent remember to keep those sandals and towels handy.

22 PEGGY'S POND

Distance ■	**11 miles (round trip)**
Hiking time ■	6 to 7 hours or 2 days
Starting elevation ■	3360 feet
High point ■	5600 feet
Hikable ■	July through September
Maps ■	Green Trails 176 Stevens Pass; USGS Mount Daniel and The Cradle
Information ■	Cle Elum Ranger District, Wenatchee National Forest, 509-674-4411 (ask about Trails 1345 and 1375)

High alpine flowers, several small alpine lakes, and a loop trip: The only tough decision to make is when to do this trip and whether to do a multiday backpack trek or swallow it all in a single day.

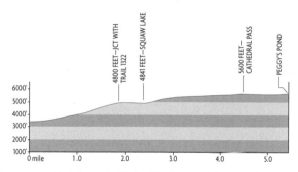

From Interstate 90, take exit 80 for Roslyn and Salmon la Sac and follow Bullfrog Road for 2.8 miles to the junction with State Route (SR) 903. Turn left onto SR 903 (sometimes called Salmon la Sac Road) and drive 16.5 miles, following signs to Salmon la Sac Campground. When the road shrinks to one lane near the campground, drive 0.1 mile and turn right onto Forest Service Road (FS) 4330 toward Tucquala Lake. Follow FS 4330

Below Cathedral Pass the Pacific Crest Trail looks down on spectacular Deep Lake. (Photo by Alan L. Bauer)

for 12.3 miles, past Tucquala Lake on the left, to the Tucquala Meadows trailhead near the road's end.

Cathedral Rock Trail 1345 crosses a bridge over the Cle Elum River and soon heads uphill beneath a heavy forest canopy that provides blissful shade on a hot August day. The first 1.8 miles include a series of broad switchbacks that carry hikers to 4800 feet and a junction with Trail Creek Trail 1322. Another gentle 0.7 mile leads to the shores of 4841-foot Squaw Lake, a worthy stop for anyone on his first backpacking trip and one of the few campsites in the vicinity with year-round water.

Beyond the lake, the trail climbs steadily another 2 miles up to 5600-foot Cathedral Pass and a junction with the Pacific Crest Trail 2000. The pass is a great place to stop, enjoy the views and, if a 9-mile round trip is to your liking, turn back toward your vehicle. Camping is possible here but difficult because of a lack of water.

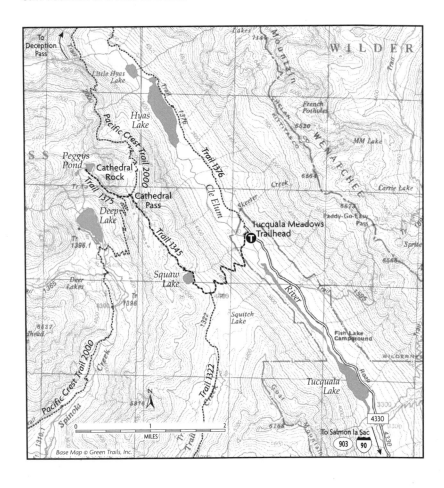

If you can handle another mile on a narrow, unmaintained trail, head for Peggy's Pond. The path is clear and no scrambling is involved, but you must feel comfortable on a narrow trail with steep exposure and usually a few downed trees.

From Cathedral Pass, head left toward Deep Lake, walking 0.3 mile of the Pacific Crest Trail, then turn northwest onto primitive Trail 1375 toward Peggy's Pond. The path to the pond follows 0.7 mile of nearly level trail that skirts the western edge of 6724-foot Cathedral Rock. Campsites are available around the pond and near its smaller, unnamed pool a bit downstream.

Hikers who arrive at Peggy's Pond in August are often treated to a spectacular flower show, as well as swarms of insects. Both the blossoms and the bugs decline after Labor Day, and hikers can often enjoy a relatively peaceful September at Peggy's Pond before snows return in October.

Despite its isolation, Peggy's Pond can be a busy camp full of people chasing different pastimes. Rock climbers will be heading up to enjoy the special beauty of Cathedral Rock, while mountaineers trudge off to climb 7899-foot Mount Daniel. Those who prefer less sweaty pursuits can simply sit back and enjoy views of both peaks.

Most day hikers and backpackers head back from Peggy's Pond the way they came, a round trip that totals 11 miles. Those with more ambition and time can create a loop by heading north once they return to Cathedral Pass. The Pacific Crest Trail will take them 5.2 miles to 4475-foot Deception Pass, where they can follow Trail 1376 south past Hyas Lake back to the Tucquala Meadows trailhead. With the Peggy's Pond detour included, the loop totals 16.7 miles.

23 DAVIS PEAK

Distance ■	**10.8 miles (round trip)**
Hiking time ■	5 to 6 hours
Starting elevation ■	2630 feet
High point ■	6426 feet
Hikable ■	Mid-July through September
Maps ■	Green Trails 208 Kachess Lake; USGS Davis Peak
Information ■	Cle Elum Ranger District, Wenatchee National Forest, 509-674-4411 (ask about Davis Peak Trail 1324)

Hikers can always tell which trails were built by people in a hurry, and the path up Davis Peak is a classic example. Leisurely strolls were not on the minds of the people who pioneered this calf-cramping route up to what was once a fire lookout. Still, the lookout builders knew where to find good views, and modern-day hikers willing to sweat (it is hot) and strain (it is steep) will be rewarded with a stunning panorama.

From Interstate 90, take exit 80 for Roslyn and Salmon la Sac and follow Bullfrog Road for 2.8 miles to the junction with State Route (SR) 903. Turn left onto SR 903 (sometimes called Salmon la Sac Road) and drive 16.5 miles, following signs to Salmon la Sac Campground. When the road shrinks to one lane near the campground, drive 0.1 mile and turn right onto Forest Service Road 4330 toward Tucquala Lake. Follow this washboard gravel for 1.6 miles, then turn left at the sign for Davis Peak Trail 1324. A large parking lot sits 0.4 mile down this dirt road; park passenger vehicles here. Stout rigs with high ground clearance can go another 0.2 mile to a smaller parking lot next to the trailhead.

Trail 1324 descends to a footbridge across the rushing Cle Elum River and, amid a slightly confusing tangle of social shortcuts, begins an uphill trudge that lasts virtually the duration of the hike. The trail's elevation-gaining pitch starts out as steady, soon increases to steep, and in places rises to "What were they thinking?"

Views are limited for the first 1.5 miles, but then the low-growing shrubs and thick canopy of Douglas fir thin to reveal the forested hillsides to the south. By the time hikers have switchbacked up to 3700 feet, Cle Elum Lake has become visible. Views improve with each uphill step, and soon the thinning trees make room for alpine flowers such as magenta paintbrush and blue lupine.

Around 5300 feet, the trail crosses a stony swath left by decades of crumbling rock, a spot where lingering snow often covers the trail well into July. Snow also can be a problem about a mile from the summit when the trail levels out briefly to traverse a forested bowl with a particularly sheltered north-facing slope.

The final mile switchbacks up a mostly exposed ridge until it reaches the grassy meadow just below the summit that once held the fire lookout. Little remains here other than rusted metal, charred wood, empty bottles,

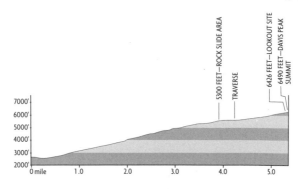

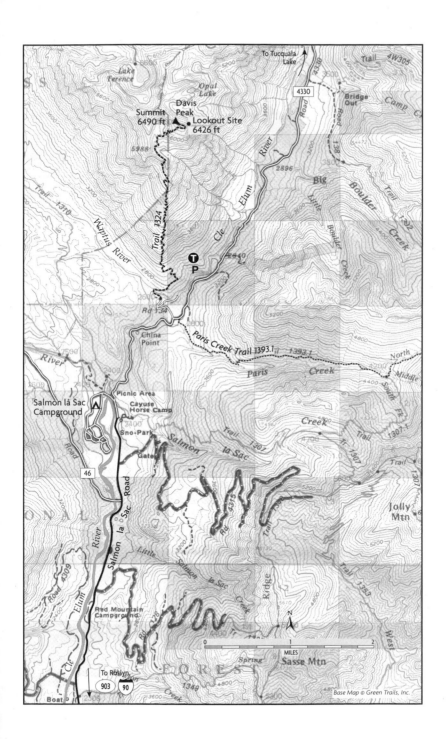

Cle Elum Lake as seen from the summit of Davis Peak.
(Photo by Skip Card)

and stones piled into a windbreak—all of which suggest the 6426-foot site still gets some use as a viewpoint. Cle Elum Lake sparkles to the south, but rugged alpine eye candy looms to the east, north, and west.

For unobstructed views, sure-footed hikers can trace the boot track to a high point somewhere along Davis Peak's horseshoe-shaped crest. The true summit tops out at 6490 feet.

TEANAWAY RAIN SHADOW

A quick glance at a topographic map should show the experienced* weather watcher why the region around the Teanaway River Valley is home to so many dry hikes.

Ridges and mountains protect the Teanaway Valley like a fortress. Incoming moisture blowing from the west first hits the Cascades crest at Snoqualmie Pass. Then it must squeeze past 7899-foot Mount Daniel. Beyond Daniel, moist winds are progressively drained by Keechelus Ridge, Kachess Ridge, Polallie Ridge, and Cle Elum Ridge. If storms blow from the north, the Teanaway region is protected by the massive Stuart Range. To the south, Easton Ridge and South Cle Elum Ridge protect the area.

In a typical year from June 1 through September 1, the Teanaway usually receives 3.3 inches of precipitation while Snoqualmie Pass gets 12.7 inches. During the dry summer of 1989, Teanaway received *no* rain from May 31 through August 19, while Snoqualmie Pass recorded 2.5 inches of precipitation.

The area is not always calm. Thunderstorms can occur during July and August, although often the storms occur without a drop of rain ever hitting the ground. Occasionally these storms are accompanied by strong winds. In the mid-1990s, gusts clocked at up to 80 miles per hour from a "microburst." Microbursts usually occur in thunderstorms. They are strong, concentrated downdrafts that emanate from storm clouds, and the winds are so strong that they have caused a number of commercial passenger jets to crash on attempted takeoffs and landings.

In addition to being dry, the scenic Teanaway region also is relatively close to major Puget Sound cities. Fast-driving Seattle residents can reach some trailheads in about an hour. The region also sees less snowfall in winter. Combined with the region's springtime sun, that means many trails will melt free of snow in May or early June, well before other regions.

* Anyone who has read this far.

Preceding page: The route to Teanaway Ridge passes by old ponderosa pines and open views. (Photo by Alan L. Bauer)

24 : LAKE ANN

Distance ■	**8.2 miles (round trip)**
Hiking time ■	4 to 5 hours
Starting elevation ■	4243 feet
High point ■	6480 feet
Hikable ■	Early July to early October
Maps ■	Green Trails 209 Mount Stuart; USGS Mount Stuart
Information ■	Cle Elum Ranger District, Wenatchee National Forest, 509-674-4411 (ask about Trails 1394 and 1226.2)

Do not get frustrated if you arrive on a summer weekend to find this trailhead parking lot crammed with cars. Hikers flock to this patch of the Wenatchee National Forest because its prime location in the heart of rain shadow territory almost guarantees no precipitation between late spring and early fall. The other reason for the popularity is that this trailhead leads to such popular places as Longs Pass, Lake Ingalls, Mount Stuart, and the rock-climbing walls of Ingalls Peaks. That is good news for those planning to hike to little-known Lake Ann, since it means 90 percent of hikers will be going in another direction.

From Interstate 90, take the State Route (SR) 970 exit (the second exit for Cle Elum) and follow SR 970 east for 7 miles. Cross the Teanaway River and turn left on Teanaway Road. Follow Teanaway Road and later North Fork Teanaway Road along the river for 12.5 miles to 29 Pines Campground. Just beyond the campground, turn right onto Forest Service Road 9737. Drive 8 miles to the end of the gravel road and the parking lot, elevation 4243 feet.

Trail 1394 follows an old mining route that in 0.4 mile reaches a junction that siphons off the traffic heading to Lake Ingalls and Longs Pass. Ignore the masses heading right and continue straight.

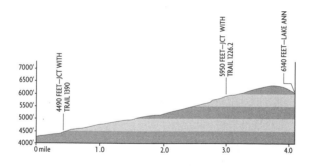

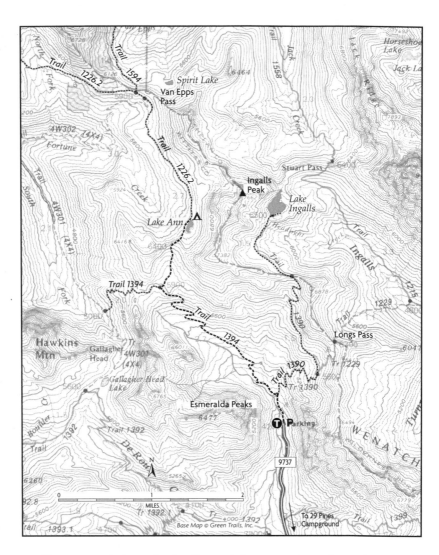

Elevation gain is gradual at first as hikers pass through ponderosa pine forest that slowly gets thinner with the rising altitude. Esmeralda Peaks rise to the left. The trail crosses several streams that can cause wet feet in June but which are often mere trickles by mid-July. Many campsites are available beside the trail for the first mile beyond the junction.

About 3.1 miles from the trailhead, hikers reach a junction where Trail

Facing page: Meadow of shooting star wildflowers along the Esmeralda Basin Trail. (Photo by Alan L. Bauer)

1394 veers west. Turn right to take the path to Lake Ann, which heads north along County Line Trail 1226.2.

Elevation gain begins in earnest after the junction, and hikers rise at least 500 feet in 0.8 mile to reach the crest of a pass. Mount Daniel rises to the west, while to the north hikers can see Glacier Peak and, beyond, Mount Baker. Not visible is a worthy campsite, since the area has virtually no flat spots and hardly a drop of water.

Hikers short of time can pause here, soak up the views, and then retrace their steps to their vehicles. Those with time (or tents) should continue down to Lake Ann, following a trail that drops 350 feet in 0.2 mile. The lake sits in a basin at 6140 feet elevation, high enough that in July the north-facing slope leading to the lake will often still have small snowfields.

The small but scenic lake is perfect for a short walk-around, and back-packers can even find some campsites not too far from shore. Campers in search of privacy often find more secluded spots about 0.7 mile to the north of the lake. However, do not expect to find seclusion from the insects, which can be thick here at the height of bug season.

Overnight visitors have several options for their return trip. Some continue another 1.75 miles along Trail 1226.2 to reach Van Epps Pass, a 5900-foot point where several trails converge. Expert mountaineers who have the necessary climbing and routefinding skills can head northeast from Lake Ann toward the saddle of Ingalls Peak. The trip is a technical scramble not recommended for novices, but the effort rewards climbers with great views of Mount Stuart and Lake Ingalls—and the crowds.

25 ┊ LAKE INGALLS

Distance	■ **10.8 miles (12 miles with side trip to Longs Pass)**
Hiking time	■ 9.5 hours
Starting elevation	■ 4243 feet
High point	■ 6500 feet
Hikable	■ Mid-July through mid-October
Maps	■ Green Trails 209 Mount Stuart; USGS Mount Stuart
Information	■ Cle Elum Ranger District, Wenatchee National Forest, 509-674-4411 (ask about Trail 1390)

Two for the price of one is the theme for this trail, which gives hikers excellent views of Mount Stuart and a grand alpine lake. Seeing it all is an ambitious undertaking covering up to 12 miles. Start early in the day to avoid the hot sun.

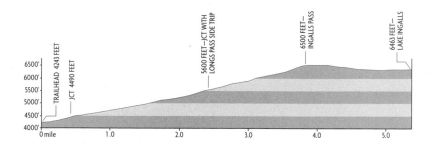

From Interstate 90, take the State Route (SR) 970 exit and follow SR 970 east for 7 miles. Cross the Teanaway River and turn left on Teanaway Road. Follow Teanaway Road and later North Fork Teanaway Road along the river for 12.5 miles to 29 Pines Campground. Just beyond the campground, turn right onto Forest Service Road 9737. Drive 8 miles of gravel road to the parking lot and trailhead, elevation 4243 feet.

The trail starts on an old mining road in an area called Esmeralda Basin. After 0.4 mile, turn right at the junction and follow Trail 1390 east toward Lake Ingalls and Longs Pass. This trail gains elevation quickly, rising in 2 miles from 4490 feet to 5600 feet. To avoid dwelling on the warm sun and your burning calves, scan the ground for green-colored serpentine rocks, whose minerals are used to make asbestos.

The Esmeralda Peaks appear to the south as the trail works its way up the hillside, and hikers also can gaze down the Teanaway River Valley. At the junction 2.4 miles from the trailhead, the path forks. Trail 1229 goes to the right, northeast to Longs Pass. Trail 1390 continues northwest to Lake Ingalls.

Hikers who want to see some views (or who feel too pooped by this point to cover another 3 miles to Lake Ingalls) should head toward Longs Pass. The path is steep, rising 700 feet in just 0.6 mile, but effort pays off with what probably are the region's best views of 9415-foot Mount Stuart, the craggy crown of the Stuart Range. The 6300-foot pass offers several resting spots to take a drink, get your wind back, and enjoy the views. Return to your vehicle from here, and you will have logged 6 miles.

Most hikers feel their energy restored by the time they return to the junction with Trail 1390, so they head north toward Lake Ingalls. The path heads steadily uphill, and at 6000 feet Mount Rainier appears above a ridge to the south. Photo opportunities increase 1.5 miles from the junction as the trail reaches 6500-foot Ingalls Pass at the crest of a ridge that defines the boundary with the Alpine Lakes Wilderness.

At this point, the sights of the entire Ingalls Creek Valley and Mount Stuart seem to be at hand's reach. Scramble up about 30 feet to the top of the ridge to take in the entire Stuart Range and Ingalls Peak, as well as

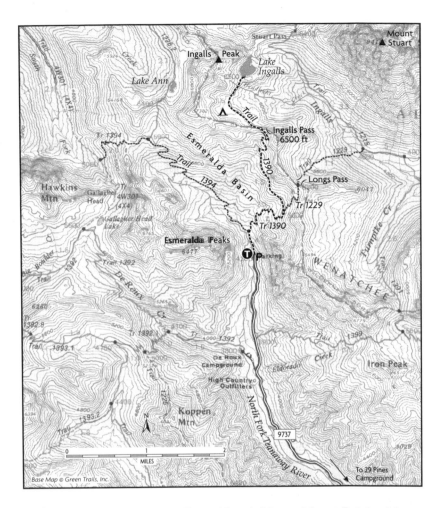

the lower basins and creek valleys. Also visible are Mount Rainier, Mount Adams, and, far in the distance, even Mount Aix and Bismark Peaks.

If time and energy are short, or if lingering snow is covering the trail, turn around here and descend 3.9 miles back to your vehicle. Hikers who took the Longs Pass scenic detour have covered 5.1 miles by this point.

Those determined to see Lake Ingalls should continue north another 1.5 miles of mostly level traveling. The final 0.2 mile involves some routefinding on a rocky slope, but pop over the top of a ridge and 6463-foot Lake Ingalls suddenly appears. In October, the fading needles of the larch coat the area in golden color. Take in the views, particularly the looming sight of 7662-foot Ingalls Peak, but also keep an eye on your watch. From the lake, it is 5.4 miles back to your vehicle.

Lake Ingalls, above 6600 feet, with Mount Stuart in the background. (Photo by Alan L. Bauer)

Backpackers can set up tents below the pass in Headlight Basin, where water and camps await. Camping is not allowed at Lake Ingalls.

26 BEAN CREEK BASIN

Distance ■	**3.8 miles (round trip)**
Hiking time ■	3 hours
Starting elevation ■	3600 feet
High point ■	5100 feet
Hikable ■	Mid-June through mid-October
Maps ■	Green Trails 209 Mount Stuart; USGS Mount Stuart
Information ■	Cle Elum Ranger District, Wenatchee National Forest, 509-674-4411 (ask about Trail 1391.1)

This low-mileage gem among the treats of the Teanaway country offers something different from spring to fall. In June, hikers can spot avalanche lilies poking through the melting snow of Bean Creek's lower basin. By July, a wide array of wildflowers coat the meadows. August brings the heat prized by sunshine seekers. Finally, September and October offer fall colors and cool nights.

Bean Creek Basin. (Photo by Alan L. Bauer)

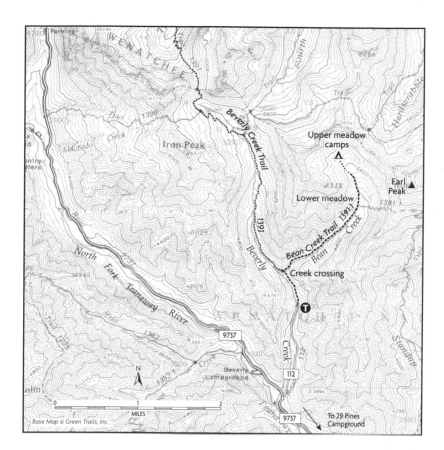

From Interstate 90, take exit 85 toward Cle Elum and follow State Route 970 east for 7 miles until the road crosses the Teanaway River. Turn left onto Teanaway River Road and go 12.5 miles to 29 Pines Campground. Just past the campground, turn right on Forest Service Road (FS) 9737. Follow this gravel road for 3.75 miles, past FS 9703 (Stafford Creek Road), and turn right onto FS 112. Continue 0.75 mile to the trailhead of Bean Creek Trail 1391.1 and Beverly Creek Trail 1391.

The trail follows an old mining road for 0.5 mile to a junction where the two creek trails split. Veer right onto Trail 1391.1, follow the path as it runs uphill beside Bean Creek, and hike a quarter-mile to the creek crossing at 3800 feet—a tricky proposition in June when the snowpack is melting out and the creek is high. Early-season hikers often carry sandals. Those who visit in July or August should not worry, since by then the creek is usually a trickle.

In typical Teanaway fashion, the trail alternates between open views through thin pine forest and deep forest along Bean Creek. Finally some

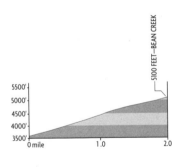

wide views open up, revealing Earl Peak and other peaks of the region.

At 1.4 miles from the junction with the Beverly Creek Trail, around 5100 feet, hikers get to make a decision in the lower meadow. Some hikers might choose to drop their packs near the creek, eat lunch, and declare this their turnaround point—a destination that will create a 3.8-mile round trip. The spot is pleasant enough for wandering. Deep forest lines Bean Creek's streambed, while a short distance away the pines thin to expose some views.

Those with enough gumption to climb a bit higher can reach more open views of the region's peaks. An unmaintained boot path heads north alongside the creek for 0.5 mile, leading hikers on a sometimes muddy path to 5600 feet elevation and Bean Creek's upper meadow. Good campsites are found here, and water is always available.

Hikers with the scrambling skills of a mountaineer can continue east on Trail 1391.1 on a rough path that leads steeply up a nearby ridge near the crest of the Wenatchee Mountains. The trail tops out about 6240 feet, a high vantage point that offers views of nearby 7036-foot Earl Peak and the more distant crags of the Stuart Range.

27 IRON PEAK

Distance	■ **7 miles (round trip)**
Hiking time	■ 3 to 4 hours
Starting elevation	■ 3920 feet
High point	■ 6510 feet
Hikable	■ Mid-June to early October
Maps	■ Green Trails 209 Mount Stuart; USGS Mount Stuart
Information	■ Cle Elum Ranger District, Wenatchee National Forest, 509-674-4411 (ask about Iron Peak Trail 1399)

Miners really did find iron around Iron Peak—just as they found gold by Blewett Pass and still pull copper from hills near Navaho Peak. Today, people trudging up the sunny hillsides more often carry trekking poles than pickaxes, and the rewards from their labors benefit the spirit more

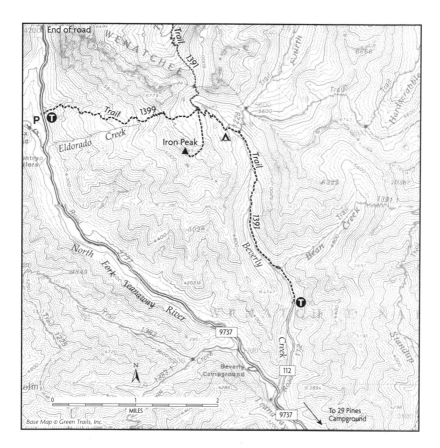

Base Map © Green Trails, Inc.

than the wallet. Among the most profitable rewards for a good day of leg-work are the views from atop Iron Peak.

From Interstate 90, take exit 85 toward Cle Elum and follow State Route 970 east for 7 miles until the road crosses the Teanaway River. Turn left onto Teanaway River Road and go 12.5 miles to 29 Pines Campground. Just past the campground, turn right on Forest Service Road (FS) 9737. Follow this gravel road 9 miles and look for a small parking area on your left, across the road from the trailhead on your right. (If you reach the end of the road, you have gone about 1.1 miles too far.)

Iron Peak Trail 1399 gets busy quickly, gaining 1700 feet in the

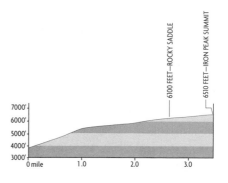

first 2 miles of steady switchbacks. Snow is rarely a problem, since the trail runs up a southwest-facing slope that melts out in early summer. Views improve with elevation, and soon hikers can see the Esmeralda Peaks, Koppen Mountain, and other peaks to the west.

The trail crests after 2.5 miles at a rocky saddle, elevation 6160 feet. A

Views of Mount Stuart and the Stuart Range from the trail to the summit of Iron Peak. (Photo by Alan L. Bauer)

faint boot path leads 1 mile to the 6510-foot summit of Iron Peak. The views from atop Iron Peak are superb, highlighted by the massive granite slab of 9415-foot Mount Stuart. Look below the peaks to see the vast spreading hillsides and ridges of the Teanaway region.

Good overnight campsites can be found just off Trail 1391, along Beverly Creek about 0.8 mile south of the junction with Trail 1399. Those who left a spare vehicle on FS 112 at the Beverly Creek trailhead (starting point for Hike 26) can continue south to complete a 7-mile one-way trek.

28 INGALLS CREEK

Distance ■	**11.4 miles (round trip)**
Hiking time ■	5 to 6 hours
Starting elevation ■	1950 feet
High point ■	3440 feet
Hikable ■	May to October
Maps ■	Green Trails 210 Liberty and 209 Mount Stuart; USGS Liberty and Mount Stuart
Information ■	Leavenworth Ranger District, Wenatchee National Forest, 509-548-6977 (ask about Ingalls Creek Trail 1215)

A 1950-foot trailhead elevation makes the Ingalls Creek Trail popular among hikers itching to log some boot mileage when most mountain trails are still snowed in. Yet hikers who venture along this creekside trail in mid-May and early June (or earlier if winter snowfall has been below average) also enjoy two other pleasures: the roar of a river brimming with snowmelt, and a profusion of alpine wildflowers trying to soak up some sun.

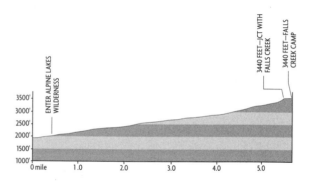

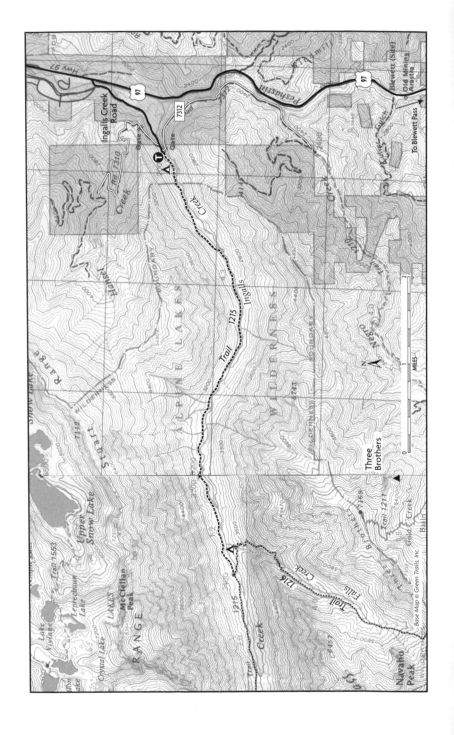

Drive US 97 north 12 miles beyond Blewett Pass (sometimes called Swauk Pass) and watch for Ingalls Creek Road. Turn left on Ingalls Creek Road and drive almost a mile to the end of the road and the trailhead. Ingalls Creek Trail 1215 runs eastward along the north side of Ingalls Creek, following a parallel path that rarely lets the river out of its sight. The first 0.5 mile of the trail previews what is in store for this grand early-season flower show. Glacier lilies spread across vast areas amid the ponderosa pines, and later in spring and summer come trillium, golden paintbrush, queen's cup, and other blossoms.

Elevation gain is gradual—roughly 250 feet in altitude for every linear mile—and parents hiking with small children can find a good campsite a little less than a mile up the trail. Campers should remember they crossed the boundary into the Alpine Lakes Wilderness about 0.4 mile up the trail, so campfires are not permitted and other earth-friendly rules apply.

Continue up the trail, slowly gaining elevation as you drink in the sights and sounds of this V-shaped river valley. Peaks in the craggy Stuart Range—a natural boundary between the Alpine Lakes and Enchantment Lakes areas—rise like guard towers to the north. Smaller peaks and foothills loom to the south, and in many places small streams trickle down gullies to fortify Ingalls Creek.

Snow often dictates how far hikers can comfortably go. In May, people often lose sight of the trail at about the 4-mile mark, and anyone not fluent in the language of routefinding should let conditions dictate their turn-around point. By late May, most hikers can comfortably get as far as Falls Creek and, just west of where the two creeks collide, the full 5.5 miles to the junction with Falls Creek Trail 1216. Falls Creek Camp is on the south side of the river, 0.2 mile beyond the trail junction; use extreme caution when crossing the river when spring snowmelt is at its peak.

For those who camp here, a day-trip option is to head south up the Falls Creek Trail and then veer off trail to scramble up to the crest of the Three Brothers, a three-headed ridge with a high point of 7303 feet. The scramble is a lot of work, and water in the area is limited, but the reward is one of the best views of Mount Stuart and an excellent chance at grabbing some scenic solitude.

As June melts into July, the Ingalls Creek Trail clears for its full length and gives backpackers several long-haul options. Some hike 12.2 miles from the original trailhead to the junction of Trail 1229, veer south another 1.1 miles to Longs Pass, then drop down for 3 miles to the parking lot at the end of North Fork Teanaway Road—where, with planning, another vehicle awaits.

Serious mountain climbers stay on Trail 1215 and hike to 6400-foot Stuart Pass—a full 15.5 miles from the trailhead—to gain access to 9415-foot Mount Stuart. If climbing is not your style, continue over the pass to Jack Creek Trail 1558 (Hike 19) and hike 12 more miles along the creek to Icicle Creek Road and recreation options in the Leavenworth area.

Warning: Ticks are becoming a springtime problem in some areas of this region, and in summer watch out for the western rattlesnake.

Ingalls Creek roars with spring runoff in May. (Photo by Alan L. Bauer)

29 MILLER PEAK

Distance ■	**8 miles (round trip)**
Hiking time ■	5 hours
Starting elevation ■	3200 feet
High point ■	6402 feet
Hikable ■	Late June to early October
Maps ■	Green Trails 209 Mount Stuart and 210 Liberty; USGS Mount Stuart
Information ■	Cle Elum Ranger District, Wenatchee National Forest, 509-674-4411 (ask about Trail 1379)

Miller Peak loses some of its majesty as spring fades to summer and the 6402-foot peak sheds its snowy cloak. By the time the snow is gone, Miller blends in with the other Teanaway mountains and pales when compared to the dramatic crags of the Stuart Range. Hikers who have muscled up the summit trail's 3200 vertical feet know the reward is not so much where you sit but what you see. Once atop the peak, hikers might feel they are on top of the world.

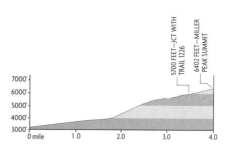

In July wildflowers grace the last stretch of the Miller Peak Trail before the summit. (Photo by Alan L. Bauer)

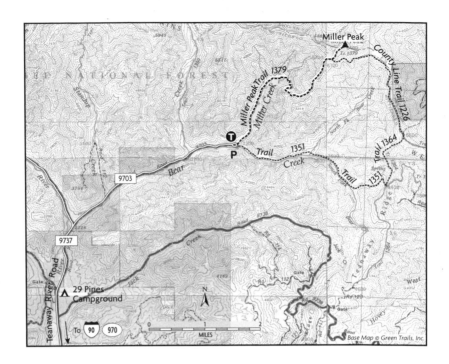

From Interstate 90, take exit 85 toward Cle Elum and follow State Route 970 east for 7 miles until the road crosses the Teanaway River. Turn left onto Teanaway River Road and go 12.5 miles to 29 Pines Campground. Just past the campground, turn right onto Forest Service Road (FS) 9737. Go 1.25 miles and turn right on FS 9703 (Stafford Creek Road). Proceed 3.5 miles on FS 9703 to the end of the road and the parking lot for Trails 1379 (detailed here) and 1351 (Hike 30).

Trail 1379 begins moderately, following a gentle grade alongside (and sometimes across) Miller Creek. Hikers gain 800 feet in the first 1.8 miles before the path steepens and the serious legwork begins.

After 3.6 uphill miles, the path reaches a junction with Trail 1226, known as County Line Trail because its path straddles the Kittitas–Chelan boundary. Veer left to stay on Trail 1379 for a final calf-cramping summit push that rises 700 feet in 0.4 mile.

The panoramic views from Miller Peak's summit are some of the best in the area, revealing all the major peaks in the rugged Teanaway landscape. Hikers also get an unobstructed view of Mount Rainier, the Stuart Range, Mount Daniel, and the vast sweep of the Columbia Basin region. It is a perfect spot to pull out the map and plan the rest of your summer and fall hiking itinerary.

A look at the map also will reveal several options for your return. Many choose to create a loop hike: From the junction of Trails 1379 and 1226, turn left and follow Trail 1226 east and south for 2.8 miles to a 5500-foot intersection with Trail 1364. Turn right onto 1364 for 1.4 miles, then turn right again at Trail 1351 for a 3.5-mile descent back along Bear Creek to the parking lot. If this is too long or too complicated, from the summit just head back the 4 miles you came.

30 ■ IRON CREEK TO TEANAWAY RIDGE

Distance ■	**6.4 miles (round trip)**
Hiking time ■	3 to 4 hours
Starting elevation ■	3800 feet
High point ■	5489 feet
Hikable ■	Mid-May until October
Maps ■	Green Trails 210 Liberty; USGS Liberty
Information ■	Cle Elum Ranger District, Wenatchee National Forest, 509-674-4411 (ask about Trail 1351)

Tired of snow, clouds, and drizzle on the trails near Snoqualmie Pass? Eager to put away your skis and break in your new hiking boots? Then you will appreciate the topographical differences of the trail along Iron Creek. The surrounding region gets 34 percent of Snoqualmie's snow, and the south-facing slope soaks up enough springtime sun that it often melts out by mid- to late May. Views aren't bad, either.

From Interstate 90, take exit 85 near Cle Elum and follow State Route 970 to the connection with US 97. Follow US 97 north and, 5.8 miles south of Blewett Pass (sometimes called Swauk Pass), look for easy-to-miss

The Teanaway Ridge Trail crosses a narrow ridge line just north of the Iron Bear Trail-Bear Creek Trail junction. (Photo by Alan L. Bauer)

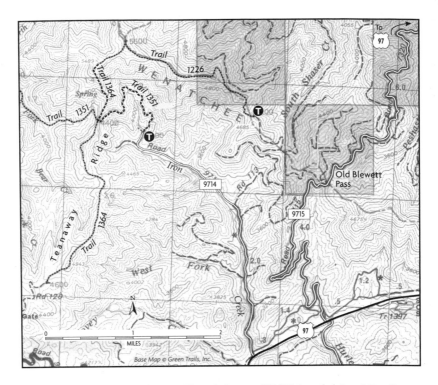

Base Map © Green Trails, Inc.

Forest Service Road (FS) 9714. Turn left onto FS 9714 and drive 3.5 miles to the trailhead near the end of the road.

The first mile of Trail 1351 is lined with flowers tucked amid the rocks, and hikers who visit in late May or June should see an abundance of balsamroot, lupine, and paintbrush. After 1.8 miles, the trail reaches a crossroads with Teanaway Ridge Trail 1364 and Bear Creek Trail 1351. Turn right onto Trail 1364 and hike north along Teanaway Ridge. If the day is hot, stop here, pull up a log, and enjoy the view of Mount Daniel to the west.

From the junction, Trail 1364 grinds uphill another 1.4 miles and gains another 1090 feet to reach an unnamed 5489-foot knoll on Teanaway Ridge.

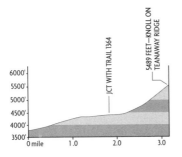

Here Mount Stuart and its backups in the Stuart Range stand directly before your eyes, while Mount Rainier looms to the south.

From here, hikers can rest, relax, and head back to the vehicle, but the tangle of trails on the ridge offers several options. For a different perspective on Mount Stuart, hike back to the junction but continue south on Trail 1364 for another

1.2 miles along Teanaway Ridge. A viewpoint here offers better sight lines of Stuart's surrounding peaks. To return, retrace your steps and turn right at the junction with Trail 1351.

Hikers organized enough to arrange a two-vehicle shuttle can leave one at the trailhead for County Line Trail 1226. To get there, turn off US 97 onto FS 9715 (the old Blewett Pass highway) and navigate your way amid the tangle of side roads to the County Line trailhead. This trailhead is often tricky to find, and the roads have few signs to help drivers navigate, so allow time for routefinding.

A more complicated option is to leave a second vehicle at the end of Stafford Creek Road, starting point for Bear Creek Trail 1351. (For directions, see Hike 29 to Miller Peak.) From the junction on Teanaway Ridge, hikers can follow Trail 1351 for a leisurely 3.5 downhill miles.

31 TRONSEN RIDGE

North Portion

Distance ■	9.8 miles (round trip)
Hiking time ■	4 to 5 hours
Starting elevation ■	4640 feet
High point ■	5800 feet
Hikable ■	Late May through late October
Maps ■	Green Trails 210 Liberty; USGS Blewett Pass

South Portion

Distance ■	8 miles or more (round trip)
Hiking time ■	4 to 5 hours
Starting elevation ■	5680 feet
High point ■	5800 feet
Hikable ■	June through late October
Maps ■	Green Trails 210 Liberty; USGS Blewett Pass

Information ■	Leavenworth Ranger District, Wenatchee National Forest, 509-548-6977 (ask about Trail 1204 along Tronsen Ridge)

Walk a ridge above tree line for an entire day. Stay in constant view of the Stuart Range, Mount Rainier, the Eastern Washington desert environment, and more than fifty-five varieties of wildflowers. It does not get much

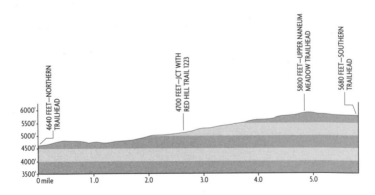

better than this. While most hikes offering such scenery require hikers to start low and gain thousands of feet, the Tronsen Ridge Trail lets hikers step directly onto the ridge to hike the 5.8-mile-long trail. You even get your choice of two trailheads. *The only caution:* The ridge is constantly exposed to the hot Eastern Washington sun. Bring plenty of water, and start early in the day if possible.

NORTH PORTION

To reach this trailhead requires a truck or sport utility vehicle with four-wheel drive. From Interstate 90, take exit 85 and follow US 97 over Blewett Pass (also called Swauk Pass). Five miles north of the pass, turn east off the highway onto Forest Service Road (FS) 7224, labeled "Five Mile Road." Drive along gravel and dirt for 3.2 miles, avoiding the side roads. Watch for a spring that runs down the roadway about 0.3 mile from the trailhead. The well-marked trailhead area, elevation 4640 feet, has ample parking and makes a worthy car camp.

Gorgeous views begin immediately at this trailhead, and hikers can gaze at Mount Stuart while they lace up their boots. The scenery only gets better once hikers hit Trail 1204 and head south. Wildflowers will often be in bloom along the entire hike from mid-May through most of June, and hikers can sometimes see completely different ecosystems within 50 feet of one another. A rocky area might contain sage, bitterroot, Tweedy's lewisia, and a large patch of Lyall's mariposa lily. Just downhill from this might be a lush forest of grand fir, Douglas fir, and spruce surrounded by grassy ground cover.

If the brilliant wildflowers are blinding, then look up at the surrounding ridges, mountains, and valleys. To the east lie Devil's Gulch, Mission Ridge, the Columbia River region of Wenatchee, and the Waterville Plateau. To the west is the entire Teanaway Mountains area and the full Stuart Range. Northward lies 10,541-foot Glacier Peak and surrounding mountains. Hikers also are likely to see ample signs of elk and even black bear.

There is no real destination along Tronsen Ridge, just plenty of good

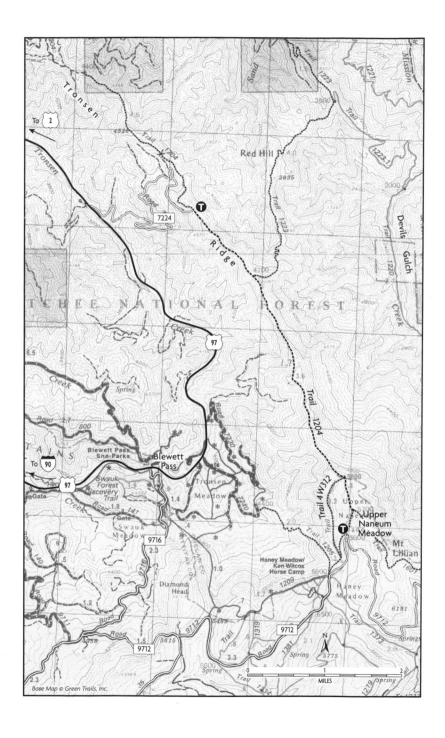

places to stop and enjoy the views when the mood strikes. Many hikers turn around after 4 miles, but those with ambition and stout legs can travel 5.8 miles to the Upper Naneum Meadow trailhead, at the starting point of the ridge's southern section.

Tronsen Ridge's northern section often appeals to hikers because its lower elevation melts free of snow earlier in summer. The northern area also is less popular with motorcyclists, who are allowed on the trail from June 15 through October 1. Those who return in October are greeted by stands of larch trees turning a gorgeous gold.

Tronsen Ridge becomes covered in wildflowers, such as these lupines, in springtime. (Photo by Alan L. Bauer)

SOUTH PORTION

Four-wheel drive helps here, too. At the crest of Blewett Pass, turn south off US 97 onto FS 9716. Follow FS 9716 for 2.75 miles, turn left onto FS 9712, and head east 4.25 miles to the Haney Meadow area, site of several trailheads. Continue another 0.5 mile to a stream crossing. You may need to leave passenger vehicles here at elevation 5600 feet. Four-wheel-drive rigs can sometimes be taken left up the primitive road for another 0.5 mile to Upper Naneum Meadow and a 5680-foot junction with Tronsen Ridge Trail 1204.

Hikers who start here and head north start with a bit of uphill hiking but then enjoy a gradual downhill slope along the ridge crest. The path toggles between the crest's east and west sides, alternating between views of Mount Rainier and Mount Stuart. Elevation here is higher than on the northern section of the ridge, so snow lingers longer and most flowers bloom in the first or second week of July.

Most hikers travel 4 miles, to the 4700-foot junction with Red Hill Trail 1223. Here they find a good resting place, enjoy the views, then head back uphill to their vehicles.

32 ¦ NAVAHO PASS

Distance ■	**12 miles (round trip)**
Hiking time ■	5 to 6 hours
Starting elevation ■	3100 feet
High point ■	6000 feet
Hikable ■	Mid-June though mid-September
Maps ■	Green Trails 209 Mount Stuart; USGS Enchantments
Information ■	Cle Elum Ranger District, Wenatchee National Forest, 509-674-4411 (ask about Trail 1359)

Like many areas in the Teanaway region, Navaho Pass can be buried in snow for much of the winter, blasted by freezing wind or engulfed in fog. Parts of this hike are inaccessible from the time snow begins piling up in late autumn until the first major meltout in mid-June. Come late spring or early summer, the Teanaway area becomes an oasis where hikers can often flee the rain for a dose of sunshine. By the peak summer months of July and August, the region can become so hot that smart hikers time their trips to avoid the worst of the midday sun.

From Interstate 90, take the State Route (SR) 970 exit and follow SR 970 east for 7 miles. Cross the Teanaway River and turn left onto Teanaway Road.

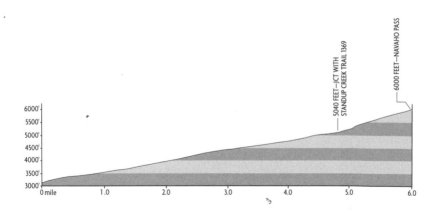

Follow Teanaway Road and later North Fork Teanaway Road along the river (stopping occasionally for views of snowcapped Mount Stuart) for 12.5 miles to 29 Pines Campground. Just beyond the campground, turn right onto Forest Service Road (FS) 9737. Drive 1.25 miles on this gravel road, turn right on FS 9703 (Stafford Creek Road), and go another 2.5 miles to the Stafford Creek trailhead, elevation 3100 feet.

Trail 1359 starts in the shade of the forest and follows alongside Stafford Creek. This trail has been rerouted several times because of washouts, and

The hike to Stuart Pass includes views of open meadows and the Stuart Range. (Photo by Alan L. Bauer)

hikers can see the old trail below them. At 4.8 miles is a junction with Standup Creek Trail 1369. Go right, staying on 1359, and continue another 1.2 steep miles to Navaho Pass, elevation 6000 feet.

Four trails converge here. Hikers who continue north on Trail 1217 descend alongside Cascade Creek to Ingalls Creek (Hike 28), which flows eastward along the base of the Stuart Range. Heading west, hikers can follow a primitive

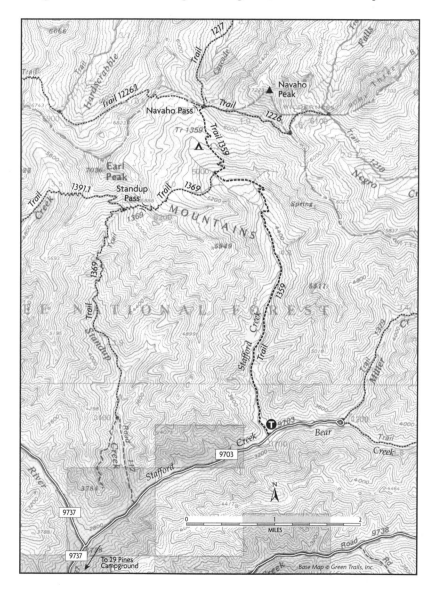

path (Trail 1226.1) up and over a ridge running north from 7036-foot Earl Peak. Those skilled at navigation can head east along Trail 1210 toward Negro Creek and can veer north off the trail to reach 7223-foot Navaho Peak. This off-trail scramble gains 1200 feet in 1.5 miles and is not recommended for anyone traveling alone or uncomfortable with low-level rock climbing.

Most hikers are content to make Navaho Pass their turnaround point. The site offers excellent views of peaks on the eastern edge of the Stuart Range, a sizable wall of granite spires that form a backdrop to the scenic Enchantment Lakes area to the north.

The pass also is a good resting place to plan for the remainder of the trip. Backpackers who expected to camp overnight will find that Navaho Pass, while scenic, is also dry. Knowledgeable campers drop their packs south of the pass at a horse camp where water is available from a small stream.

Hikers can return the way they came, a round trip totaling 12 miles. Those who want an extra workout and extra views on the return can head west at the junction with the Standup Creek Trail 1369. This detour gains another 1200 feet en route to 6200-foot Standup Pass, an excellent vantage point for views of Mount Stuart and the rest of the Teanaway region. Although scenic, the Standup Creek Trail is not as well maintained as the Stafford Creek Trail, and several river crossings can be tricky during periods of heavy snowmelt (typically May and June). The trail also spits out hikers at a different location, forcing a 3-mile walk along the road unless a spare vehicle has been parked at the Standup Creek trailhead.

33 NORTH FORK TANEUM CREEK/ TANEUM RIDGE

Distance ■	**14 miles (loop)**
Hiking time ■	6 to 7 hours
Starting elevation ■	3100 feet
High point ■	4250 feet
Hikable ■	Late May through September
Maps ■	Green Trails 240 Easton and 241 Cle Elum; USGS Cle Elum, Frost Mountain, Ronald, and Quartz Mountain
Information ■	Cle Elum Ranger District, Wenatchee National Forest, 509-674-4411 (ask about Trails 1377, 1378, 1363)

You might be the only hiker on this scenic trail in the forests south of Cle Elum, but you will hardly be alone. Trails in this section of the Wenatchee

National Forest were often designed for two-wheeled traffic, and people who brave these paths on foot quickly learn to make room for motorcycles and mountain bikes. Hikers willing to sniff a bit of blue exhaust will be rewarded with a scenic loop in which the moments between the motor noise offer creeks, meadows, forests, and some wide-open views. Those who arrive midweek or in late spring when snow still lingers on the trail might have the place to themselves.

From Interstate 90, take exit 84 for Cle Elum and South Cle Elum. Turn south at the Cle Elum information center at the sign for South Cle Elum, then drive under the freeway, over the Yakima River, and straight through town. Follow the road as it elbows left and becomes Lower Peoh Point Road. Turn right at the intersection with Upper Peoh Point Road, drive 1 mile, then turn right onto Mohar Road. Follow Mohar for 2 miles until it meets Westside Road. Turn left onto Westside, drive 0.1 mile, then turn left onto the gravel of South Cle Elum Ridge Road (also known as Forest Service Road 3350). Drive 6.6 miles up to a five-way intersection and take the easy right onto Forest Service Road (FS) 119. Follow FS 119 for 2.7 miles to the trailhead marked by a sign for Trail 1377.

The trail begins amid dense stands of lodgepole pine on a sloping hillside above the North Fork of Taneum Creek, which at first can be heard but not seen. The trail rises and falls for a mile until it puts hikers close enough to actually touch the creek, and beyond that the water is rarely more than a stone's toss from the path. The creekside setting is pleasant but somewhat monochrome. The biggest scene changes come as hikers pass close to logged-out parcels of private land.

The soundscape can change more abruptly, particularly when hikers meet some of the many motorcyclists who use this trail. Smart hikers learn to quickly jump to one side of the trail when they hear an approaching two-stroke engine—regardless of who has the legal right of way. Many motorized travelers on these trails use hand signals to announce if others are coming behind them, so the biker who looks like he is flashing a peace sign is actually telling you that two more dirt bikes are on their way.

After roughly 4 miles, hikers reach the first of six wooden bridges that crisscross the meandering North Fork of Taneum Creek. At 5.2 miles is the junction with Trail 1378, which runs up to Fishhook Flats. Day hikers al-

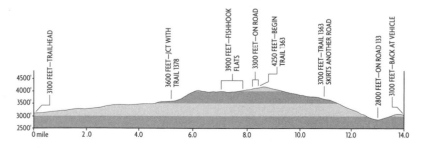

ready pooped by this point should turn around and return the way they came, because the biggest elevation gain lies directly ahead.

Hikers who still have some steam in their legs can create a loop hike by following Trail 1378. Turn left at the junction onto Trail 1378, which crosses the river and begins an uphill journey. The trail rises steadily and sometimes steeply from the junction, elevation 3600 feet, to a tiny hilltop clearing at 4170 feet elevation, a worthy rest stop. The pines are thick here, but peekaboo views of the Stuart Range are possible. If not, enjoy the lupine, trillium, bear grass, and Oregon grape at your feet.

The trail drops to about 4000 feet, crosses a creek, rises again, then alternately falls and rises until hikers reach the meadows of Fishhook Flats. Grass and other low-growing greenery replace trees in this 3900-foot marsh, where hikers stand a fair chance of spotting any elk that have not been spooked by the dirt bikes.

The trail rises steadily beyond the flats until it joins FS 3300. To this point, hikers have covered 8.2 miles of mountain trail without seeing any significant mountain views. That soon changes. Turn left on the road, walk on the

Hiker Gary Jackson enjoys a lunch stop along the North Fork Taneum Creek. (Photo by Alan L. Bauer)

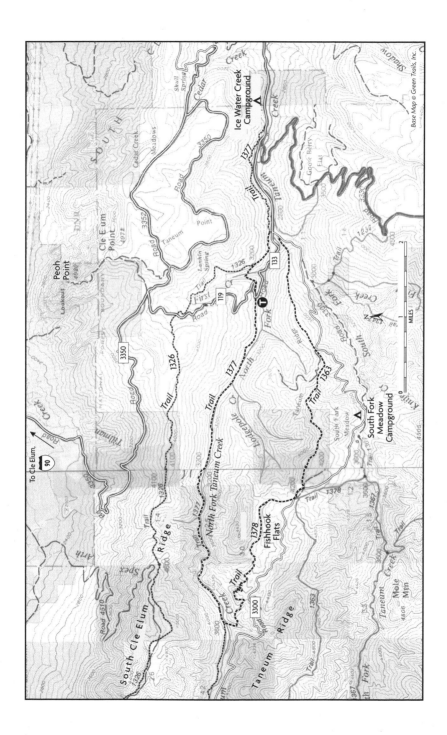

Base Map © Green Trails, Inc.

gravel for about 0.2 mile, turn left onto Taneum Ridge Trail 1363, and in a few paces the mountainside vistas open wide. This is partly because Trail 1363 traces the crest of an exposed ridge, but it is mainly because most of the view-blocking trees have been cut and turned into two-by-fours.

The ridge trail is so wide at first that hikers might think they are on a dirt road rather than a trail, but in time the path narrows and begins a winding descent back amid the trees. Another road appears after 2.5 mostly downhill miles; Trail 1363 skirts the road but does not cross it. The path then rises slightly before making a steady and often steep 1.7-mile descent to a roadside trailhead.

Hikers who by now have had their fill of dirt paths can walk 0.1 mile to join FS 133, turn left, and trudge directly up the road to their vehicles. Those who prefer life on the trail can walk 0.1 mile to the road, cross to Trail 1377 on the other side, then hike up it. Follow this road for 0.6 mile, turn left at the junction with Trail 1326, then rise and fall another 0.8 mile back to your vehicle.

MOUNT RAINIER
RAIN SHADOW

efore the arrival of European explorers, the indigenous locals often called Washington's highest peak Takhoma, Tahoma, or Ta-co-bet. These names mean "Big Mountain," "Snow Peak," or "Place Where the Waters Begin." The names worked fine until Captain George Vancouver sailed past in 1792 and named the snowcapped mountain after a local brand of beer.

No, seriously, he named the peak after his sailing buddy, Rear Admiral Peter Rainier, a rather portly guy with thick glasses who fought against the Americans during the Revolutionary War. Many locals—indigenous and otherwise—have been miffed ever since.

At 14,410 feet, Mount Rainier is so big that its very presence often creates unsavory weather that sends hikers and climbers scrambling for their Gore-Tex. But a big peak casts a big rain shadow. Since wind with storms primarily sweeps in from the southwest, the driest rain shadow regions around the peak will be northeastern spots such as Corral Pass, Noble Knob, and Norse Peak. Areas farther west such as Burroughs Mountain and Grand Park are not quite as dry.

However, Rainier's rain-stopping profile never guarantees a dry hike. The area around Corral Pass, for example, usually has more than a hundred inches of snow on the ground in the middle of winter. Still, the rain shadow hikes listed here offer a solid statistical chance of seeing less moisture than areas on the Rainier's wet western side. Paradise might see 3 inches of rain on a soggy summer day, but Corral Pass might receive only 1 inch.

Hmmm . . . we're not selling this very well. Try this: On a summer day when Paradise is overcast and coated in light drizzle, Corral Pass and the Sunrise region will be sunny. Sound better? Then hike on.

Preceding page: The summit of Crystal Peak offers stunning views of Mount Rainier. (Photo by Skip Card)

34 KELLY BUTTE

Distance ■	**2.6 miles (round trip)**
Hiking time ■	1.5 hours
Starting elevation ■	4500 feet
High point ■	5409 feet
Hikable ■	July through October
Maps ■	Green Trails 239 Lester; USGS Lester
Information ■	Enumclaw Ranger District, Mount Baker–Snoqualmie National Forest, 360-825-6585 (ask about Trail 1031 to Kelly Butte Lookout)

Some might scoff at the idea of a rain shadow so close to the Cascades crest, or a suggested hike that lasts a mere 1.3 miles one way, but the trail to the old lookout atop little-known Kelly Butte has the rainfall figures and scenery to merit a recommendation. The butte is perfectly positioned so southwest winds lose their moisture when they hit Mount Rainier. The site's 5409-foot perch offers excellent views, particularly when Rainier is bathed in a cloud cap. *But hikers beware:* The trail is not maintained and

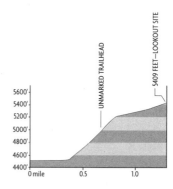

The short hike up Kelly Butte offers spectacular views of Mount Rainier. (Photo by Dennis Long)

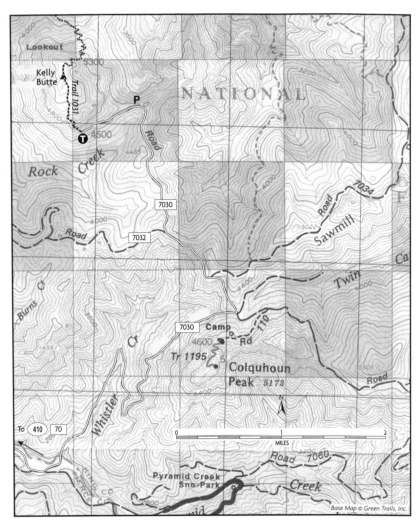

Base Map © Green Trails, Inc.

can get very rough in places. Anyone who ventures here without a good road map risks getting lost in the tangle of winding gravel.

From State Route 410, find Forest Service Road (FS) 70, located 2.3 miles east of Greenwater. Turn onto FS 70 and drive 8.5 miles east to FS 7030. Turn left onto FS 7030 and follow it as it curves 8.2 miles through forest amid a tangle of turnoffs. The trailhead sits at the end of the road, but the final 0.75 mile goes from bad to worse and is suitable only for rugged vehicles with high clearance. What's more, there's very little space for turning a vehicle around. For most vehicles, a wide flat spot beside the road is the preferred parking spot.

From the parking area, walk the last 0.75 mile along the road and look for the unmarked Trail 1031 on the right. Head up this steep path, and be alert for loose gravel and slippery footing. For the difficult first 50 yards, one needs to be skilled and comfortable in scrambling up this loose terrain. Another caution is that this trailhead is difficult to find, so it will be necessary to carefully study the maps before you head here. The hike is worth the fuss, but we strongly suggest you consider the difficulties before you tackle its challenges. The trail becomes more reasonable beyond here, although hikers will still face steep sections and minor switchbacks.

Views open up once hikers reach the lookout, a still-standing relic of the days before fires showed up on satellite images. With luck—and perhaps some volunteer efforts—the structure will be restored and preserved rather than torn down

35 | GRAND PARK

Distance ■	**Up to 19 miles (round trip)**
Hiking time ■	8 to 10 hours or 2 days
Starting elevation ■	6385 feet
High point ■	6800 feet
Hikable ■	Late July through early October
Maps ■	Green Trails 270 Mount Rainier East; USGS Sunrise
Information ■	Mount Rainier National Park, 360-663-2273 (ask about the Grand Park Trail)

The 2-mile-long meadow of Grand Park provides a rare bit of flat terrain amid Mount Rainier's otherwise turbulent topography. Wildflowers and wild views make this long trek worthwhile, even though tired hikers will face most of their elevation gain on the return trip.

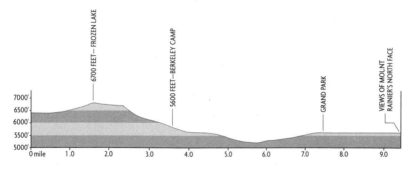

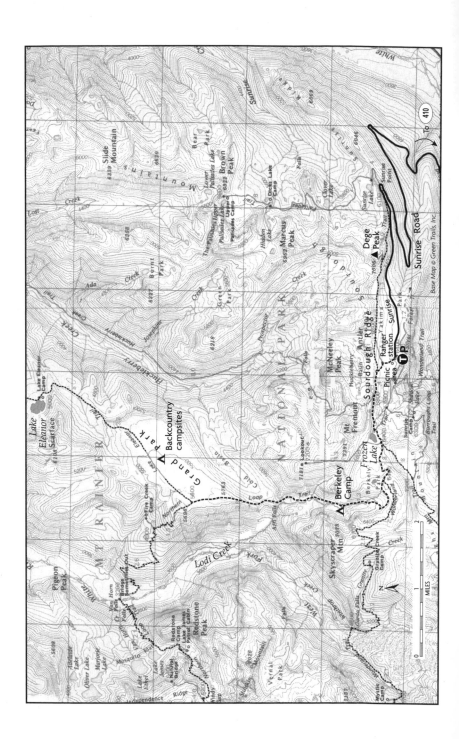

The Grand Park Trail passes through flower-filled meadows with exceptional views of Mount Rainier. (Photo by Alan L. Bauer)

Drive to the northeast corner of Mount Rainier National Park from State Route 410 and turn west into the park's White River entrance. Pay at the entrance booth a mile from the turnoff, then continue another 13 miles up to Sunrise. Drivers should keep their eyes on the road during the winding approach, but passengers can enjoy watching Mount Rainier come into view, followed by distant Mount Adams. Trail maps are available at the Sunrise Ranger Station.

The trail to Grand Park begins amid a confusing tangle of Sunrise footpaths and, most likely, a horde of wide-eyed tourists. The confusion and crowds fade with distance. From the ranger station, head north toward the picnic area and, in 0.2 mile, look for a junction. Head left toward Sourdough Ridge (avoiding the right turn to Dege Peak) and walk another 0.2 mile to reach the ridge trail. Head left again, walk 1 mile west to Frozen Lake, and in another 0.2 mile look for a junction and the trail toward Berkeley Camp.

Marmots often whistle to travelers on this section of trail, part of what the park calls the Northern Loop. The trail here descends steadily, dropping from 6700-foot Frozen Lake down to 5600-foot Berkeley Camp in 2.1 miles. From Berkeley Camp, it is 3.8 undulating miles north to the unmistakable flat meadow of Grand Park. By the time hikers reach the junction at the head of the meadow, they have covered 7.5 one-way miles.

Grand Park's flat terrain—a rarity in the up-and-down world around Mount Rainier—formed when lava filled a prehistoric canyon. Today, the tabletop meadow is a favorite place for visitors to catch the wildflower displays of late July or early August, or to catch the reds of autumn when the ground cover turns in September. The only bad time to come to Grand Park is winter, when the area lies blanketed in snow, or early spring, when the meltout turns the meadow to a marsh.

Those who wander 2 miles north through the meadow have their backs to the best view, so after going in a bit, turn around to face Mount Rainier's forbidding north face. During silent moments, hikers might hear boulders tumbling down the steep, jagged face of the Willis Wall.

Camping is permitted at Grand Park only for those who demonstrate the proper skills (and attention to rules) to earn a special backcountry permit. Most overnight guests stay instead at Berkeley Camp so they can spend the full day in Grand Park's meadow. Water is limited at the camp in late August, so travel prepared.

36 BURROUGHS MOUNTAIN

Distance ■	**6.6 miles (round trip)**
Hiking time ■	3.5 hours
Starting elevation ■	6385 feet
High point ■	7402 feet
Hikable ■	Late July through early October
Maps ■	Green Trails 270 Mount Rainier East; USGS Sunrise
Information ■	Mount Rainier National Park, 360-663-2273 (ask about the trail to Burroughs Mountain)

The power of Mount Rainier's glaciers is obvious from Burroughs Mountain, which offers the best seat in the house to take in the massive Emmons Glacier and its neighbor, the Winthrop. Hikers also can see the avalanche-scarred Willis Wall and steep Liberty Ridge, areas with some of Rainier's most challenging climbing routes. Mileage is moderate and elevation gain is manageable, but most of the ascent will come near the hike's end.

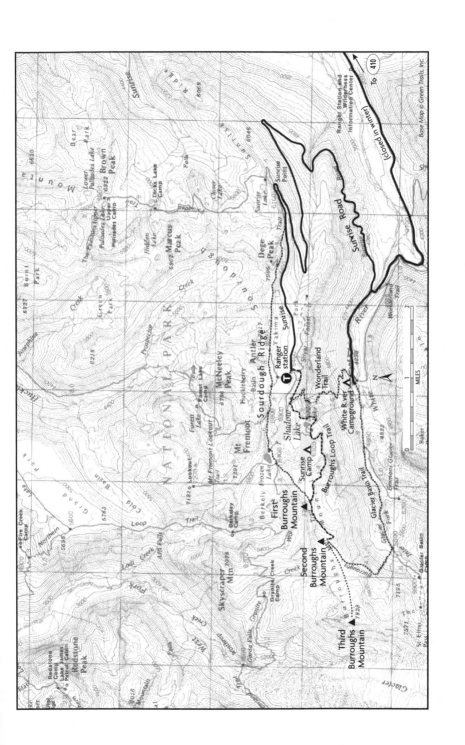

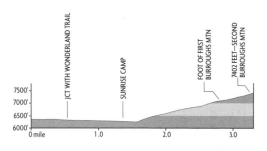

Drive to the northeast corner of Mount Rainier National Park from State Route 410 and turn west into the park's White River entrance. Pay at the entrance booth a mile from the turnoff, then continue another 13 miles up to Sunrise.

The hike begins on the south side of the Sunrise parking lot where hikers pick up a gentle westward path that skirts a steep hillside and offers good views of Rainier's Emmons Glacier. At 0.5 mile, the path reaches a junction with the mountain-encircling Wonderland Trail; stay right, avoiding a left turn down a steep path, and continue another 0.9 mile to Sunrise Camp.

At the junction of the Wonderland Trail and the trail to Sunrise Camp, turn off the Wonderland Trail onto the Burroughs Loop Trail, where the serious elevation gain begins. A junction 1.4 miles farther puts hikers at the foot of First Burroughs Mountain. Turn left (avoiding the right turn to Frozen Lake) and head uphill another 0.5 mile to Second Burroughs Mountain.

From this moonscape of open slopes and pumice, hikers have a box seat for Mount Rainier's glacial slide show, but these slow-moving rivers of ice are not the only forces that shape the mountain. Near Steamboat Prow (the triangle-shaped wedge of rock that splits the Emmons and Winthrop Glaciers), hikers can see orange hillsides that were scarred about 5600 years

The trail to Burroughs Mountain crosses tundra-like landscape for most of the way. (Photo by Alan L. Bauer)

ago by the massive Osceola Mudflow. Debris from this flow traveled down the White River Valley toward Puget Sound, burying land that today sits beneath Enumclaw and Orting.

Hikers will have covered 3.3 miles to reach this point. Those who crave more wandering can continue southwest on the Burroughs Mountain Trail and head down and over on an unmaintained path that goes due west to Third Burroughs Mountain, elevation 7828 feet.

Those who were organized enough to leave a spare vehicle at the White River Campground can stay on the trail and switchback down the steep path to the Glacier Basin Trail. Once the joint-pounding descent is over, the trail covers 2.4 gentle downhill miles along the White River to the campground. To reach the White River Campground, turn left at the sign 4.1 miles from the entrance booth and drive 1.5 miles to the camp.

37 HIDDEN LAKE

Distance ■	**6.4 miles (round trip)**
Hiking time ■	3 to 4 hours
Starting elevation ■	6100 feet
High point ■	6100 feet
Hikable ■	Mid-July through mid-October
Maps ■	Green Trails 270 Mount Rainier West; USGS White River Park
Information ■	Mount Rainier National Park, 360-663-2273 (ask about Palisades Lakes Trail from Sunrise Point and side trail to Hidden Lake)

Virtually all hikes in Mount Rainier National Park start with the idea that views will improve with elevation. The trail to Hidden Lake turns this concept on its head, sending hikers down a scenic valley dotted with alpine lakes separated by rolling rows of forested ridges. Hidden Lake is an after-thought for most who follow what park officials call the Palisades Lakes Trail, but the scenic detour leads hikers to one of the park's hidden jewels. Those who visit see one of the park's highest yet least advertised alpine lakes, and they also get a rare Rainier opportunity for some scenic solitude.

To reach the trailhead, follow State Route 410 to the northeast corner of

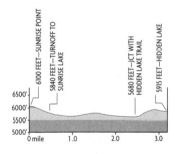

Mount Rainier National Park and turn near milepost 62 toward the park's White River entrance. Pay admission at the entrance booth a mile down the road, then drive another 11 miles to Sunrise Point, elevation 6100 feet. Park in the lot inside the hairpin curve, and look for the trailhead for the Palisades Lakes Trail near the bend in the road.

The trail initially heads eastward along Sunrise Ridge but soon curves west and descends steeply into the valley. The turnoff to Sunrise Lake is reached after 0.4 mile, and soon after the trail bottoms out at 5500 feet—the lowest point in this hike.

Hikers continue up a low ridge then descend to 5732-foot Clover Lake. Another up-and-down mile leads to a spot near Tom, Dick, and Harry Lakes where hikers find the junction with the trail to Hidden Lake.

The trail starts at 5680 feet and rises quickly about 300 feet in 0.3 mile before cresting the ridge that hides Hidden Lake from the rest of the valley. The trail drops down and wraps around the southern edge of the 5915-foot lake, ending where the lake's western edge butts against a steep bowl.

Stay a respectful distance from the fragile lakeshore, and avoid wandering

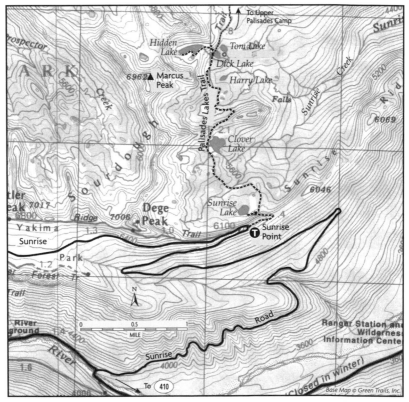

Hidden Lake lies in a basin framed by steep hillsides of rocky scree.
(Photo by Skip Card)

in areas where boot-beaten meadows are being restored. Instead, find a comfortable perch and drink in views of the high walls of fir-dotted scree and towering rock that frame Hidden Lake's northern shore. Steep hills covered in trees and alpine flowers surround the lake's other sides like a circular amphitheater, but a gap to the east provides a picture window with blue-sky views stretching toward Eastern Washington.

Near the end of the maintained trail at the western edge of Hidden Lake sits an unmaintained trail that heads steeply up the eastern hillside to some high alpine meadows. All unmaintained trails should be treated with caution, for they often contain unmarked obstacles and other hazards. For most hikers, the lake is a worthwhile end of the trail.

38 SLIDE MOUNTAIN

Distance ■	**11.4 miles (round trip)**
Hiking time ■	5 to 6 hours
High point ■	6339 feet
Starting elevation ■	6100 feet
Hikable ■	Mid-July through September
Maps ■	Green Trails 270 Mount Rainier West; USGS White River Park
Information ■	Mount Rainier National Park, 360-663-2273 (ask about Palisades Lakes Trail from Sunrise Point and unmaintained path to Slide Mountain)

Few scenic destinations on the popular paths of Mount Rainier National Park offer much in the way of wilderness solitude. Not surprising, really, since the

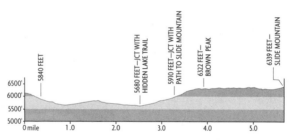

park has to put its 2 million annual visitors somewhere, and they can't all fit in the Paradise Visitor Center. Yet, hikers can often find some elbow room on the unbeaten path to Slide Mountain, a seldom-visited peak tucked away in the obscure Sourdough Mountains. *But be warned:* The trail follows an unmaintained boot track that demands solid routefinding skills, and the region is lonely enough that any lost or injured hiker could wait a long time for help. Wise hikers will trek close enough to see but not touch Slide Mountain.

To reach the trailhead, follow State Route 410 to the northeast corner of Mount Rainier National Park and turn near milepost 62 toward the park's White River entrance. Pay admission at the entrance booth a mile down the road, then drive another 11 miles to Sunrise Point, elevation 6100 feet. Park in the lot inside the hairpin curve, and look for the trailhead for the Palisades Lakes Trail near the bend in the road.

The trail starts eastward along Sunrise Ridge but soon curves westward and descends into a valley filled with small lakes. A turnoff to Sunrise Lake appears after 0.4 mile, slightly larger Clover Lake appears just over a mile later, and the junction with the trail to Hidden Lake (Hike 37) a mile after that. Another 0.8 mile of scenic walking brings hikers to Upper Palisades Lake, elevation 5910 feet, and the end of the maintained trail.

The easy-to-miss turnoff for the faint boot track toward Slide Mountain

The rock formation known as The Palisades looms over much of the trail to Slide Mountain. (Photo by Skip Card)

comes about 0.1 mile before the trail's end, right around the point hikers get their first distracting glimpse of Upper Palisades Lake. The unmaintained path's first 0.5 mile heads upward at an impossibly steep pitch toward 6322-foot Brown Peak, an excellent viewpoint and a good turnaround for people uncomfortable going farther.

The trail skirts Brown Peak's summit to trace the crest of a high ridge separating Lower Palisades Lake from the marshy meadow of Bear Park. The ridge offers excellent views and is another good turnaround for hikers uncomfortable on the unmaintained boot track. Beyond, the path heads north another 2 miles, mostly uphill, skirting a ridgeline punctuated by three unnamed but distinctly different peaks. The first is coated in grass and stunted trees, the second has a steep eastern flank of pale red and gray scree, and the craggy third has slopes littered with slabby rocks that have crumbled from its summit.

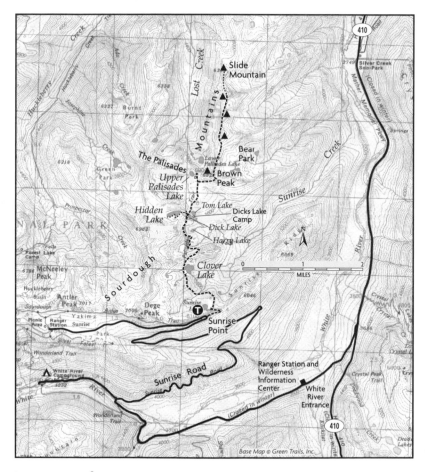

Few venture this far into Rainier's untracked territory, and many who do stop well short of Slide Mountain in favor of one of the three peaks on the approach. The final 0.5 mile to Slide Mountain is particularly treacherous—an unstable ridgeline of large, tilting slabs where a false step can lead to a snapped ankle or other serious injury. Use extreme caution. Better yet, do not do it, since the three peaks on the approach are all better destinations. All rise several hundred feet higher than Slide, and reaching the top of the 6620-foot peak in the center of the trio barely requires a scramble.

Regardless of where you stop, the views are spectacular. Mount Rainier and its dominant Emmons Glacier steal the show, but hikers can also spot Mount Adams to the south and sometimes Mount Baker to the north. Fans of rock (the mineral, not the music) will enjoy the gnarled columns of the Palisades rising west of Lower Palisades Lake, while students of glacial history will appreciate the perfect U-shaped valley that lies at their feet.

Return the way you came, being careful not to veer off the boot path onto one of the many game trails created by Rainier's herds of elk and goat. (Slide Mountain is isolated, not uninhabited.)

39   NOBLE KNOB

Distance ■	**7.4 miles (round trip)**
Hiking time ■	4.5 hours
Starting elevation ■	5700 feet
High point ■	6011 feet
Hikable ■	July to early October (access road gated until road melts out)
Maps ■	Green Trails 239 Lester; USGS Noble Knob
Information ■	Enumclaw Ranger District, Mount Baker–Snoqualmie National Forest, 360-825-6585 (ask about Trail 1184 to Noble Knob)

The large rain shadow cast by Mount Rainier means the region around Noble Knob gets about half the precipitation that falls at Paradise and other parts of the mountain's wet western slopes. But Rainier's shadow is long enough—and Noble Knob high enough—that hikers should never expect perfect weather conditions. Fog is a particularly common occurrence, particularly in the mornings. At least the flowers love the moisture.

From State Route 410, find the turnoff to Forest Service Road (FS) 7174, located 12 miles east of Greenwater or 1.5 miles west of Crystal Mountain Boulevard. Head east on FS 7174 for 5.7 steep miles, following signs to

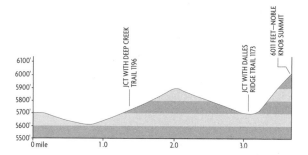

Corral Pass. The parking area for Trail 1184 is near the crest of the pass, just short of Corral Pass Campground.

Trail 1184 begins high enough that hikers need to cover little elevation before they are tracing the crest of Dalles Ridge. Views of Mount Rainier are excellent. Blooming lupine and other wildflowers line the ridge's hillsides in July.

An easy 1.4 miles bring hikers to a junction with Deep Creek Trail 1196, an alternative approach when the high trailhead is snowed in. Veer right and continue along Trail 1184, gliding along Dalles Ridge for 1.7 scenic miles to a junction with Dalles Ridge Trail 1173. Stay on 1184 for another

Views are virtually continuous along the Noble Knob Trail toward Mount Rainier. (Photo by Alan L. Bauer)

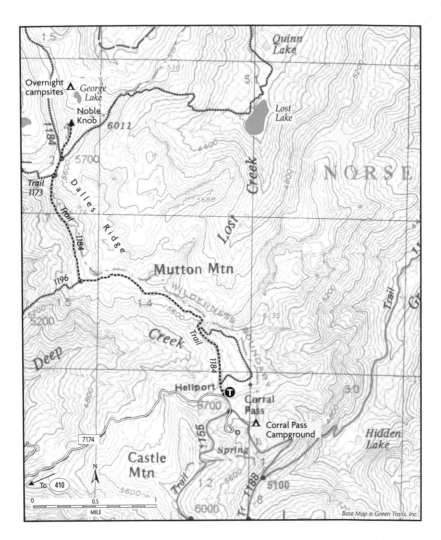

0.2 mile until you reach a three-way junction, then follow the middle fork the final 0.4 mile up to the 6011-foot summit of Noble Knob.

Mount Rainier will be in your face on the knob, site of an old fire lookout. The peak's lofty elevation makes it the high ground for much of the surrounding terrain. If you can peel your gaze away from The Big One rising up from the southwest, look east and south to take in the sweep of the scenic Norse Peak Wilderness. At your feet to the north lies George Lake, a good destination for an overnight backpacking trip.

Numerous other trails in the vicinity make worthy day trips, and a drive-in campsite at the Corral Pass Campground makes a good base for exploration. Bring water; the campground has no piped-in source.

A final caution: The road up to Corral Pass remains gated near the bottom until the area melts free of snow and the roadbed dries, usually in early July. When the snows return in October, the road closes for winter. Eager hikers with solid leg muscles can reach the area via Deep Creek Trail 1196 or Ranger Creek Trail 1197, both of which begin around 3000 feet from trailheads close to State Route 410.

40 ┆ NORSE PEAK

Distance ■	**11.2 miles (round trip)**
Hiking time ■	5 to 6 hours
Starting elevation ■	4000 feet
High point ■	6856 feet
Hikable ■	Late June to early October
Maps ■	Green Trails 271 Bumping Lake; USGS Norse Peak
Information ■	Naches Ranger Station, Wenatchee National Forest, 509-653-2205

Most hikers give the views from the summit of Norse Peak a solid-gold rating. It's good someone found gold here, since most of the miners who prospected the area for placer gold around 1900 did not strike it rich. Today, a wealth of scenery awaits hikers willing to pick their way up a long and often hot uphill path.

From State Route 410, find the turnoff to Crystal Mountain Boulevard near the boundary of Mount Rainier National Park, about 33 miles east of Enumclaw. Drive 4.3 miles up the road and turn left onto Forest Service Road 7190-410, the gravel road often used to access the Gold Hills Cabins. Drive 0.2 mile to the trailhead parking lot, located near Sand Flat Horse Camp.

Trail 1191 heads steadily uphill toward the site of an old fire lookout, rising nearly 3000 feet over 5.6 miles over an exposed slope. The trail often melts free

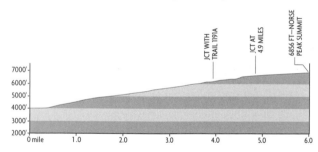

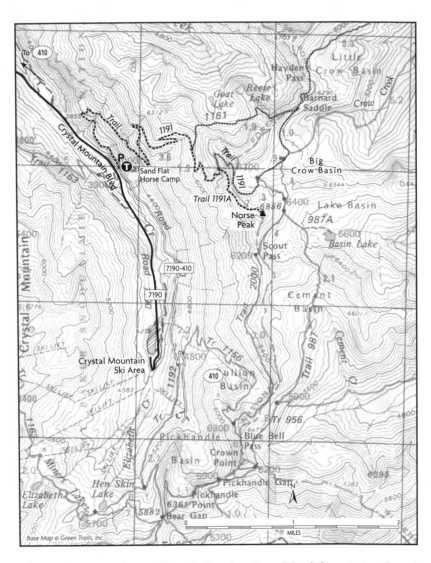

Base Map © Green Trails, Inc.

of snow far sooner than trails at similar elevations. Wise hikers start early and drink plenty of water during what is often a hot, dry slog.

Pine forests along the trail thin as hikers gain elevation, and soon views of Mount Rainier begin to poke through the trees. Also visible are the treeless hillsides of the nearby Crystal Mountain Ski Area, open meadows that erupt each July with a show of lupine, paintbrush, and other wildflowers.

After 4.9 uphill miles, hikers reach a junction where Trail 1191 splits with Trail 1191A. Take the right fork onto 1191A and head the final 0.7 mile to

Crystal Mountain Ski Area as seen from the Norse Peak Trail.
(Photo by Alan L. Bauer)

Norse Peak's 6856-foot summit. At the end of the trail, lie back and enjoy the dramatic display of Northwest mountains. From here hikers can see Mount Adams, the Stuart Range, Glacier Peak, Mount Baker, the Olympics, and, looming over them all, massive Mount Rainier.

On the way back, hikers with extra energy can turn at the junction with Trail 1191 for a side trip to Big Crow Basin, a good base for backpackers seeking an overnight campsite. Big Crow Basin features a shelter built in the 1930s by Civilian Conservation Corps crews, and water is usually available from the headwaters of nearby Crow Creek.

41 ┆ CRYSTAL PEAK

Distance ■	**7.6 miles (round trip)**
Hiking time ■	3.5 hours
Starting elevation ■	3520 feet
High point ■	6610 feet
Open and hikable ■	July through September
Maps ■	Green Trails 270 Mount Rainier East; USGS White River Park
Information ■	Mount Rainier National Park, 360-663-2273 (ask about the trail to Crystal Peak)

The phrase "360-degree view" is often overused in descriptions of hikes, since some chunk of any panorama usually does not command much attention.

But the stunning view from Crystal Peak comes close to perfection. Hikers who slog up this 6610-foot pinnacle on the eastern edge of Mount Rainier National Park might spend their peak moment pondering which way to point the camera—and then fretting they did not save enough film to record all the wildflowers they noticed on the approach.

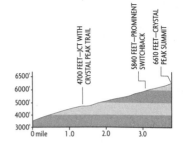

The trailhead sits off State Route 410, about half a mile north of the turnoff to Mount Rainier's White River entrance. Hide all valuables in your vehicle, as the roadside parking lot is getting a reputation for car clouts. Hikers visiting this edge of Mount Rainier National Park do not have to pay park admission fees but do have to follow all park rules. Pets are not allowed on the trail, the number of overnight visitors is limited, and any backpacker planning to camp must first obtain a wilderness permit from a park ranger.

The wide trail steps over Crystal Creek and abruptly heads uphill into a thick forest of young evergreens that keep the path shaded for much of the initial journey. Tantalizing through-the-trees glimpses of Mount Rainier appear after a few switchbacks, hints of what looms higher.

The trail splits after 1.3 miles, around 4700 feet elevation, and the main path continues straight toward the campsites of Crystal Lakes. The slightly narrower Crystal Peak Trail veers right, descending briefly to cross Crystal Creek before resuming its uphill tendency. Some maps show the Crystal Peak trail as "unmaintained," but the way is obvious and the path seems to be cleared regularly of fallen logs and other debris.

Hikers break out of the thick woods at a rock-strewn slope about 0.1 mile beyond the creek, and here Mount Rainier explodes into sight. The trail passes in and out of the trees for another mile, but around 5200 feet the path emerges onto an open hillside with unobstructed sight lines to the west. Views of the mountain and the White River Valley improve with each uphill step.

Crystal Peak's steep and exposed western flank sheds most of its snow early, and wildflowers bloom around mid-July. Blue lupine, purple penstemon, magenta paintbrush, orange tiger lily, and the white tufts of blossoming beargrass mix with the yellows of cinquefoil and arnica. The steady buzz of alpine bees is often punctuated by a marmot whistle.

The uphill trail heads steadily south to 5840 feet, switchbacks north, then makes its final winding way toward the peak's crest. The proper trail ends about 80 vertical feet shy of the 6610-foot summit, near the site of an old lookout marked by a few concrete footings. Views here are excellent, but hikers with stout legs should scramble the final slippery feet up the faint trail to get the unobstructed views at the top.

Begin by looking west at Rainier and its massive Emmons Glacier, site of the mountain's second most popular climbing route. The rocky crag of Steamboat Prow splits the Emmons Glacier from the Winthrop Glacier at 9700 feet, channeling the Emmons down to what becomes the gray streamed of the White River Valley. The tree-covered mound known as Goat Island Mountain obscures most of the muddy river's headwaters, but sharp-eyed folk will spot a hillside bearing a treeless scar from the massive Osceola Mudflow that roared through the area 5600 years ago.

Pivot left to view the black spires of the Cowlitz Chimneys. Turn a bit more and see Mount St. Helens poking above the snow-fringed north

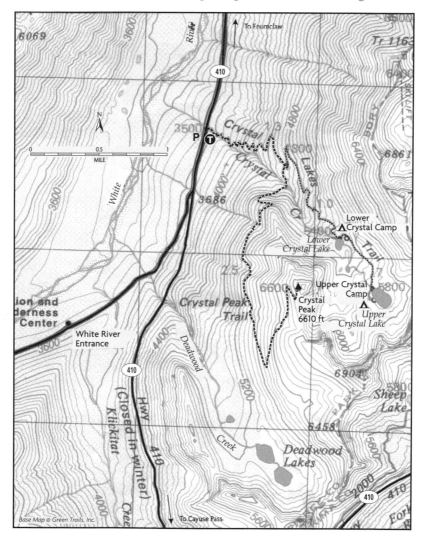

Upper Crystal Lake as seen from the summit of Crystal Peak.
(Photo by Skip Card)

slopes of the craggy Tatoosh Range. Due south in the distance stands Mount Adams, while 6220-foot Yakima Peak rises above nearby Chinook Pass. To the east, at your feet, sit the blue pools of Upper Crystal Lake and, a bit to the north, smaller Lower Crystal Lake. Both lakes lie at the base of a ridge of peaks that form the boundary between Mount Rainier National Park and the Crystal Mountain Ski Area.

The view north follows the meandering White River, and on clear days hikers can spot Mount Baker in the distance. The northwest horizon is framed by the bumpy spine of the Sourdough Mountains, including northernmost Slide Mountain (Hike 38).

Descend the way you came, but take time to smell the lupine.

*Facing page: Signpost along the trail to Goat
Peak on American Ridge.* (Photo by Alan. L. Bauer)

SOUTH CASCADES
RAIN SHADOW

Anyone who has weathered a storm on Mount Hood or Mount St. Helens knows the South Cascades can get hammered by wind and heavy precipitation. It is a funny place to stick a rain shadow.

Several factors are at work. In early fall, the shifting path of most storms (known as the "storm track") usually points at the North Cascades. While Mount Baker gets slammed, the South Cascades can remain dry well into autumn before the storm track makes an erratic but systematic migration toward California. After Californians get their winter quota of rain, the track moves north again, but by late spring it is often at the Canadian border. The state's northwest corner can get heavy rains while the southern corner often stays dry.

Geography also blesses the region, particularly the areas around Mount Adams that are shielded by big neighbors. Mount Hood squeezes some moisture out of southwest winds, while winds from the west lose moisture as they go up and over Mount St. Helens. And any wind out of the northwest will be wrung nearly dry as the air moves over Mount Rainier.

Mount Adams' extensive glaciers often disguise the relatively low rainfall in the areas around it. Tiny Trout Lake on the peak's southern approach gets 44.5 inches of rain a year. (In comparison, Mount Baker Dam, in the teeth of the storm track from the Strait of Juan de Fuca, gets 110.3 inches.)

The South Cascades cover a vast amount of territory that is diverse in topography and precipitation. The borders are Mount Rainier on the north and the Columbia River on the south. Within this region, three major volcanoes—Rainier, Adams, and St. Helens—generate their own weather.

We also include Chinook Pass, located east of Mount Rainier. Since the westerly to southwesterly winds usually prevail, hikers might think Chinook Pass would be a great place for a rain shadow. This is not the case. During most winters, the snowfall at Chinook Pass usually parallels the amount of snow at Paradise, which averages 680 inches a year.

If the rain shadow is not at Chinook Pass, where is it? Going about 5 miles east of the pass, things start to dry out. Bumping Lake, 9 miles east of Chinook Pass, gets only 48 inches of rain a year. So keep going east if you want a drier climate.

The hikes in this wide-ranging region have distinct personalities, depending on their locations. Sourdough Gap, barely east of the Cascades crest, has much in common with the trails around nearby Mount Rainier. Steep slogs, such as the paths up Fifes Ridge, Mount Aix, and Goat Peak, will challenge even strong legs. Gentler strolls through the meadows and ponds south of Bumping Lake are some of the most pleasant in the state, particularly in autumn. And the trails to Killen Creek and through the Indian Heaven Wilderness might be labeled the cream of Mount Adams' countryside.

42 ┆ SOURDOUGH GAP

Distance	■	**6.6 miles (round trip)**
Hiking time	■	3 to 4 hours
Starting elevation	■	5432 feet
High point	■	6400 feet
Hikable	■	July through early October
Maps	■	Green Trails 270 Mount Rainier East and 271 Bumping Lake; USGS Norse Peak
Information	■	Naches Ranger District, Wenatchee National Forest, 509-653-2205 (ask about Trail 2000 to Sheep Lake and Sourdough Gap)

Few hikes other than Sourdough Gap offer so much for so little uphill effort. That is probably why this snippet of the Pacific Crest Trail (PCT) is so popular and, unfortunately, so crowded. When you reach Sheep Lake, expect to see fast-moving day hikers, some novice backpackers, and probably one or two hardy PCT through-hikers bemused by this sudden brush with humanity.

The trailhead sits off State Route 410, just east of the crest of 5432-foot Chinook Pass. Two roadside parking lots are available, and overflow

Sheep Lake is the first lake you encounter on the Pacific Crest Trail north of Chinook Pass. (Photo by Alan L. Bauer)

parking can be found a short walk away on the highway's shoulders, but spaces are often in short supply on sunny summer weekends. Arrive early, and do not leave anything in your vehicle that would tempt a prowler.

This section of the Pacific Crest Trail (officially known as Trail 2000) runs northeast, parallel to and often directly above

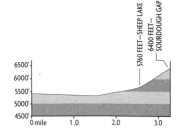

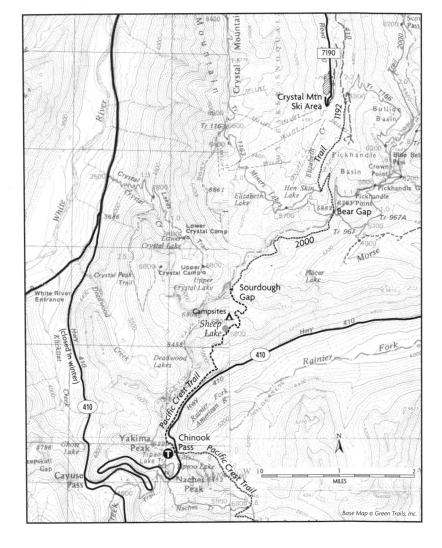

Base Map © Green Trails, Inc.

the highway, for 1.5 often downhill miles along an open, south-facing slope. Lupine and magenta paintbrush thrive on the hillside in July and August, but the roar of Winnebagos chugging up the pass somewhat dilutes what might otherwise be a wilderness experience.

After rounding a ridge, hikers turn their backs to the highway and head north up a gentle slope. Sheep Lake, elevation 5760 feet, is reached after 2.5 miles. The lake can often be crowded with overnight campers, many of them experiencing their first alpine outing. Overflow campsites can be found a short distance from the shore.

Mosquitoes also can crowd the lake prior to Labor Day. Hikers who tire of swatting bugs often quickly leave the lake, pick up the PCT on the northeastern shore, and cover another 0.8 mile of steeper trail up to 6400-foot Sourdough Gap. Views are a bit obscured here by nearby ridges; the best peeks at Mount Rainier actually come a few hundred feet below the gap.

This is the turnaround point for most day trippers. Organized hikers who remembered to leave a vehicle at Crystal Mountain Ski Area can continue north on the PCT 3.3 more miles to Bear Gap, the junction with several trails that lead down to the resort's parking lot.

43 | FIFES RIDGE

Distance ■	**10.6 miles (round trip)**
Hiking time ■	4 to 5 hours
Starting elevation ■	3330 feet
High point ■	6470 feet
Hikable ■	Late May through October
Maps ■	Green Trails 271 Bumping Lake; USGS Goose Prairie and Old Scab Mountain
Information ■	Naches Ranger District, Wenatchee National Forest, 509-653-2205 (ask about Fifes Ridge Trail 954)

Do not expect drop-dead views for all the thigh-burning muscle needed to ascend this steep ridge. But do expect a field trip that will provide lessons in geology, examples of erosion, and, just maybe, the bugle call of a love-hungry bull elk.

The trailhead sits between the Pleasant Valley and Hells Crossing Campgrounds just off State Route (SR) 410 near milepost 83. Look for the small sign for the trail, and do not be fooled by the nearby turnoff to the Fifes Peak viewpoint. A parking lot and registration box sit just off the highway.

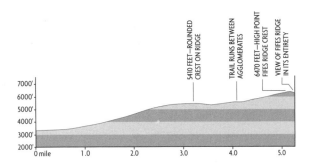

The first 0.2 mile beyond the registration box follows a dirt road suitable for sturdy SUVs but not recommended for low-clearance vehicles or trucks towing trailers. This road/trail crosses a junction with Pleasant Valley Trail 999 before the road ends and the forested footpath begins.

Level ground is abandoned after 0.5 mile as the trail veers up the hillside along Wash Creek, which can flow strong in spring but withers to a trickle in late summer. Observant hikers will see evidence of previous trails built too close to the creekbed that washed away during meltouts.

After about 2 uphill miles and several creek crossings, hikers step out onto an exposed hillside that offers a brief glimpse of Fifes Peak to the west. Following the trail back into the forest, hikers follow steep switchbacks

Rocks protrude along the rugged crest of Fifes Ridge.
(Photo by Skip Card)

and a bit of level trail until they reach a rounded crest atop a tree-covered ridge. Many stop at this 5410-foot spot to rest; the views are not great, but the trail beyond dips sharply to erase 150 feet of hard-won elevation before resuming its uphill climb.

At 4 miles, sweaty hikers look up to see the trail running between warty, three-story globs of solidified gray muck dotted with dun-colored stones. Geologists say these rock walls, known as "agglomerates," likely formed at least a million years ago (and probably much earlier) during volcanic debris flows that bound together ash and rock fragments in one muddy mass.

A few more warty towers and a stretch of very steep and often dusty switchbacks loom ahead before the trail tops out on Fifes Ridge's crest, elevation 6470 feet. Hikers can straddle the rocky, exposed ridge and gaze north across the Norse Peak Wilderness. The more interesting view, however, is found by walking a little farther to the west, where hikers can take in the entire sweep of Fifes Ridge.

Most hikers rest and recover here before turning around and retracing

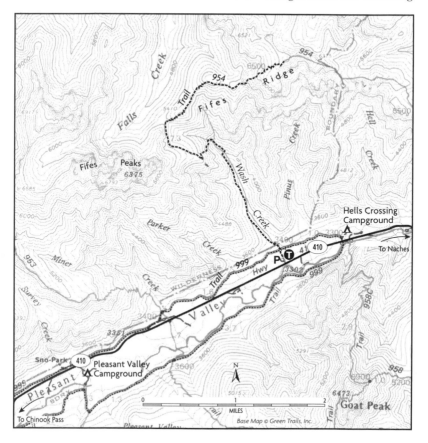

their steps—a joint-jolting exercise down hillsides that will seem steeper than they did on the uphill journey. But first, continue just a little farther beyond the highest point, where the ground's rock is a brilliant magenta and Fifes Ridge can be seen in its entirety. With this brief detour, the round trip totals about 10.6 miles.

Ambitious hikers might be tempted to continue east down the ridge and follow the trail another 9.2 miles back to an intersection with SR 410. *But be warned:* The trail gets very difficult to follow near a meadow close to the wilderness area boundary. Horse hooves, game trails, and hunters' tracks—plus a downhill hairpin turn that does not obviously correspond with most maps—make going ahead a poor option for first-time visitors without strong routefinding skills.

If hiking in autumn, be alert near the ridge top for the whistling calls of male elk looking for love. And if you hear them, also be alert for armed hunters looking for elk.

44 ┆ MOUNT AIX

Distance ■	**10.6 miles (round trip)**
Hiking time ■	3 to 4 hours
Starting elevation ■	3667 feet
High point ■	7766 feet
Hikable ■	Mid-July to mid-September
Maps ■	Green Trails 271 Bumping Lake; USGS Bumping Lake
Information ■	Naches Ranger District, Wenatchee National Forest, 509-653-2205 (ask about trails to Mount Aix)

Washington's mixed pioneer heritage has left us with some interesting place names, Mount Aix among them. A climber was once asked for the correct pronunciation of "Aix." He said, "Just remember, my body *aches* when I climb it." He wasn't joking. The trail to the 7766-foot summit of Mount Aix is not an easy hike, but alternative stopping points and side trips along the way make for a rewarding day trip.

Timing is crucial on this hike. At so high an elevation, the trail can be snow-covered well into July. In August, get an early start. The hot sun, steep trail, and south-facing hillside will increase your water consumption, and with the exception of an occasional dirty snowbank on the shady side of Mount Aix, the trail will be bone dry. Experienced hikers often wait until after Labor Day, when the temperatures start to cool.

To reach the trailhead, turn south off State Route 410 onto Bumping Lake

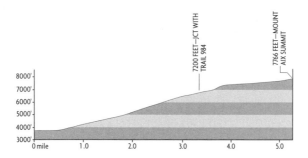

Road, which becomes Forest Service Road (FS) 1800. Drive past several good drive-in campsites until the pavement ends near Bumping Lake. Continue on FS 1800 past Bumping Lake Campground. Take the left fork onto FS 1808 and drive about 1.5 miles to the trailhead parking area, elevation 3667 feet.

Mount Aix was the site of a fire lookout, built in 1923 at a cost of $1229.53. Those bold, burly lookout builders understood that the shortest distance between two points is a straight line. True to this principle, Trail 982 does not mess around when it comes to elevation gain, rising 4000 feet in the first 3.7 miles.

Trail 982 begins mildly enough and quickly takes hikers across the

Stunning views are common along the trek up to Mount Aix.
(Photo by Alan L. Bauer)

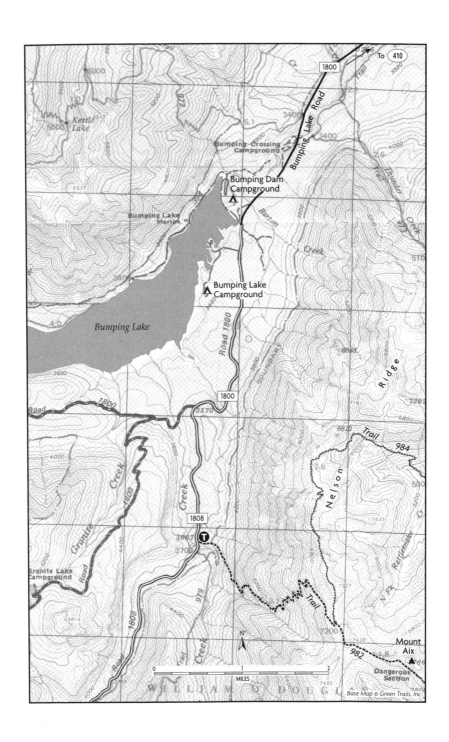

To (410)

1800

Bumping Lake Road

Thunder Creek

Kettle Lake

Bumping Crossing Campground

Bumping Dam Campground

Bumping Lake Marina

Bumping Lake Campground

Barton Creek

Bumping Lake

Road 1800

Ridge

1800

Road

Trail

Nelson

Trail

984

500

N Fk Rattlesnake Cr

Creek

1808

Granite Creek

Creek

Granite Lake Campground

Road

1808

Road

1808

Creek

N

Trail

Mount Aix

982

Dangerous Section

WILLIAM O. DOUGLAS

0   1   2
MILES

Base Map © Green Trails, Inc.

boundary into the William O. Douglas Wilderness. A long series of switchbacks promptly leads out of deep woods and into open forest. A view of Mount Rainier appears in the first mile, and vistas widen from here. In another mile the trail passes beside a small stream, creating a luxurious campsite for anyone hauling a backpack. The stream is often dry by late summer; if it is flowing, it is probably the only water source on the trail.

Not quite another mile farther, 3.7 miles from the trailhead, the trail reaches a junction with Trail 984. Views from this 7200-foot point on a clear day include Goat Rocks, Mount Rainier, and Mount Adams. For day hikers, this is a good place to have lunch and rest before the steep descent. Those who feel like wandering around for more views can head north and continue on Trail 982, a scenic path that follows along the bare crest of Nelson Ridge.

For climbers, the summit of Mount Aix lies about 1.6 miles farther east via a primitive and slightly dangerous trail that might seem relatively level considering the steep path leading up to it. Do not expect to find a fire lookout on the summit; the structure was removed in 1961, and only the foundation remains.

45 GOAT PEAK/AMERICAN RIDGE

Distance ■	6.8 miles (round trip)
Hiking time ■	5 hours
Starting elevation ■	3300 feet
High point ■	6473 feet
Hikable ■	Mid-June through October
Maps ■	Green Trails 271 Bumping Lake; USGS William O. Douglas
Information ■	Naches Ranger District, Wenatchee National Forest, 509-653-2205 (ask about Goat Peak Trail 958C)

The William O. Douglas Wilderness was named for the former U.S. Supreme Court justice who spent much of his childhood exploring this rugged and arid terrain. According to local legend, the teenage Douglas would go backpacking for days by himself. The scenic region no longer offers quite the solitude of those lonely days, but hikers who trace American Ridge can explore the region much as Douglas did and see for themselves why he loved it so much.

Drive State Route 410 about 14 miles east of Chinook Pass and park by Hells Crossing Campground on the north side of the highway, just east of a bridge over the American River. The trailhead for Trail 958C is across the road from the campground and begins at 3300 feet elevation. (Another

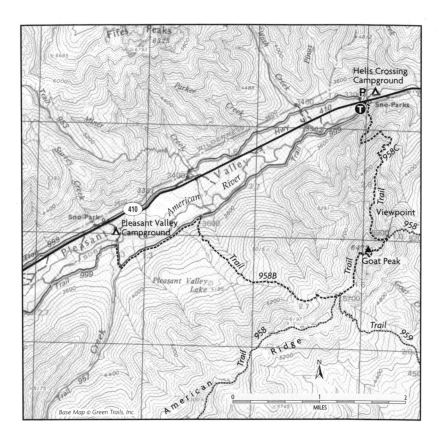

Base Map © Green Trails, Inc.

option is to begin this hike on Trail 958B, which begins farther west near the Pleasant Valley Campground. However, this requires a very difficult crossing over the American River, and there is no bridge. Snowmelt runoff can make the crossing dangerous in spring and early summer, but it is a more reasonable option in late summer or early fall.)

Hikers be warned: Water is very scarce near Goat Peak and in virtually all spots along 17-mile American Ridge. Day hikers and especially overnight backpackers should carry up all they need.

Trail 958C is a great path for those seeking some solitude and a good workout. Solitude probably comes from the fact that grand views do not appear until hikers are almost to the top of American Ridge. The workout comes from a thigh-frying grade that ascends 2600 feet in 2.8 miles.

Views open up around 5900 feet elevation as the trail nears the crest of the ridge.

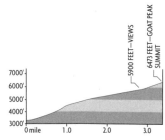

Around here, resting hikers can look north across Pleasant Valley and see the rocky ridge areas of Fifes Peak and Fifes Ridge, as well as Mount Aix, Nelson Ridge, and Bismark Peak. The ridge area also offers a spectacular flower show, and hikers can often find two species of phlox, small flowered penstemon, desert parsley, and death camas. Lower-elevation plant species include vanilla leaf, lupine, and a few calypso orchids. In fall, the trail is ablaze in vibrant yellow colors from two groves of western larch growing from 4500 feet to 5200 feet.

A short distance beyond these views lies the junction with Trail 958, which runs along the ridge crest. Turn right and head southwest, and in 0.5 mile find the spur trail on the left that heads to the top of 6473-foot Goat Peak. Here are views of Mount Rainier and Mount Adams—and perhaps a place for a nice nap.

Most hikers turn around here and head back, for a round trip of 6.8 miles. Others choose to create a loop by heading south another 1.1 mile on Trail 958 and following Trail 958B north for 2.7 downhill miles to Highway 410. Just remember the warning about the tricky river crossing near Pleasant Valley Campground.

Michael Fagin traverses an open talus slope just below the ridgeline of American Ridge. (Photo by Alan L. Bauer)

46 TUMAC MOUNTAIN

Distance	■ 7.2 miles (round trip to Tumac summit); 11.9 miles (loop with Pacific Crest Trail)
Hiking time	■ 4 hours (summit), 6 hours (loop)
Starting elevation	■ 4305 feet
High point	■ 6340 feet
Hikable	■ July through October
Maps	■ Green Trails 303 White Pass and 271 Bumping Lake; USGS Spiral Butte, Bumping Lake, and White Pass
Information	■ Naches Ranger District, Wenatchee National Forest, 509-653-2205 (ask about Trails 980, 944, 2000)

Legend says this two-headed peak was named for two Scottish sheepherders named Mac. The sheep are long gone, replaced by hikers hungry for views that take in a sweeping panorama of peaks, lakes, and forested hillsides.

The trail to Tumac Mountain begins on the path to Twin Sisters Lakes. From State Route 410, turn south near Cedar Springs Campground onto Forest Service Road (FS) 1800, following signs to Bumping Lake Recreation Area. Drive 10.8 miles to the end of the pavement at Bumping Lake, continue on the gravel for another 2.3 miles, then turn left onto FS 1808 and drive 7 miles to the trailhead at the dead end. Beware of tire-popping sharp rocks in the dirt roadbeds.

The often wide, always popular, and sometimes dusty Twin Sisters Lakes Trail 980 starts at 4305 feet and leads hikers uphill 1.6 miles through view-blocking forest to the smaller of the two twin lakes. Campsites are available here, although no overnight camps are allowed close to the fragile shore. Day hikers should be careful not to take a snack break where meadow restoration is in progress.

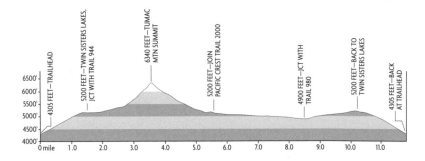

From the lake, turn left at the junction onto Sand Ridge Trail 1104 and walk through lakeside meadows coated in huckleberry bushes and dotted with small firs. After a level 0.4 mile, turn right at the "Tumac" sign onto narrow Trail 944 toward the mountain, which reveals its two-pyramid profile shortly beyond the junction.

The rutted trail passes low bushes and stubby trees on mostly level terrain for about a mile before hikers reach the base of the mountain and

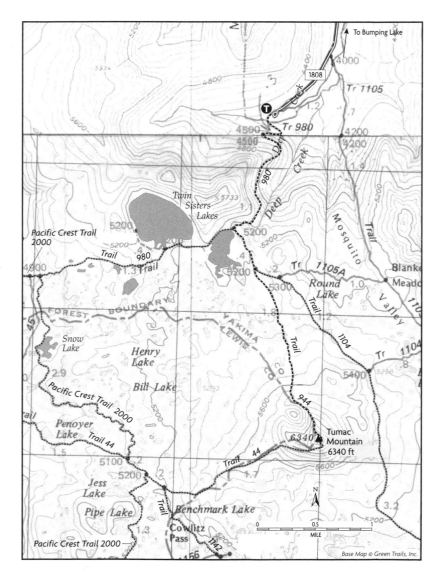

Base Map © Green Trails, Inc.

begin a steep zigzag up the final 0.7 mile. Views improve as the trail rises above the trees, eventually giving way to pumice-coated hillsides near the 6340-foot summit.

From atop Tumac, hikers can gaze in all directions at a panorama of Cascade volcanism. Dominating the western horizon is Mount Rainier, and noontime hikers with binoculars might spot climbers descending from the 14,410-foot summit along the popular Disappointment Cleaver route. (Do not look for many folks climbing up; that chore takes place at night.)

Mount Adams rises to the south, behind the snowcapped Goat Rocks and the sculpted hillsides of the White Pass Ski Area. The northern view is dominated by treeless peaks, such as 7585-foot Bismark Peak and 7766-foot Mount Aix (Hike 44). Elsewhere sits a rolling landscape of green foothills dotted with ice-blue alpine lakes, notably the Twin Sisters.

A summit register can be found in a plastic tube amid rocks near the crumbling foundation of an abandoned fire lookout. The rocks are popular resting spots, but trees near the rocks block views and make the steep hillsides just below Tumac's summit a better choice for those who want scenery with their snacks.

Many Tumac visitors return the way they came, a there-and-back journey of 7.2 miles. Hikers who want to see more of the William O. Douglas Wilderness—and get a little more exercise—can head south down Tumac Mountain along Cowlitz Trail 44 (some maps show it as Trail 944) into a shady forest. The path soon levels out and, some 1.7 miles from the summit, reaches a junction with Trail 1142.

Turn right, go another 0.2 mile, and you are on Trail 2000, better known as the Pacific Crest Trail. Head north through pristine forest and past scenic lakes, then keep right after 0.2 mile to stay on the Pacific Crest Trail when

The steep slope leading to the summit of Tumac Mountain.
(Photo by Skip Card)

Trail 44 veers west. After 2.9 mostly level miles on the PCT, turn right to join Trail 980 for a 1.3-mile uphill trudge back to the largest Twin Sister lake. Another 0.6 mile returns hikers to the smaller twin and the junction for the trail back to their vehicles. The Q-shaped journey measures 11.9 miles.

Crowds are common on these popular trails, especially on sunny weekends and particularly near the lakes. Common, too, are horse droppings left by the equestrian visitors. Courtesy and alert eyes help hikers steer clear of all obstacles.

47 | BLANKENSHIP LAKES

Distance ■	**10.7 miles (round trip)**
Hiking time ■	5 hours
Starting elevation ■	4040 feet
High point ■	5270 feet
Hikable ■	Late June through September
Maps ■	Green Trails 303 White Pass and 271 Bumping Lake; USGS Bumping Lake and Spiral Butte
Information ■	Naches Ranger District, Wenatchee National Forest, 509-653-2205 (ask about Trails 1105, 979, 1148)

When ancient cartographers wanted to keep people away from choice spots, they often scrawled "Here be dragons" on the maps. The U.S. Forest Service did the same thing by labeling the meadows near Blankenship Lakes "Mosquito Valley." Do not be repelled. Plan your trip for late summer or early fall (when the bloodsuckers are less active), pack some DEET, and visit on a slightly windy day. Then brace yourself for one of the region's most scenic blends of forest, meadows, streams, and lakes.

From State Route 410, turn south near Cedar Springs Campground onto Forest Service Road (FS) 1800, following signs to Bumping Lake Recreation Area. Drive 10.8 miles to the end of the pavement at Bumping Lake, continue on the gravel for another 2.3 miles, then turn left onto FS 1808. Follow the washboard for 6.3 bumpy miles, then turn left at the sign for Deep Creek Horse Camp and Indian Creek Trail 1105.

The trail crosses Deep Creek (often a wade for hikers who cannot find a fallen log) and then begins a steady ascent through the protected firs, hemlocks, and pines of the William O. Douglas Wilderness. Hikers can enjoy the chirps of birds, the whistles of marmots, and the splash of a nearby creek as they keep an ear cocked for the clomp of approaching horse hooves. (Trail etiquette dictates that hikers step off the trail, downhill from the horse.)

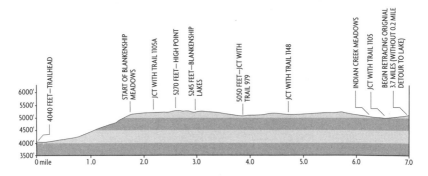

Views open dramatically about 1.9 miles from the trailhead when hikers step onto the grass of beautiful Blankenship Meadows, a long field of fir-fringed green bisected by the brown rut of the trail. Maps consider this the heart of Mosquito Valley, even though the stagnant ponds where the little vampires breed are a ways distant.

Follow the rutted trail past a hitching post (the clearest sign of the junction with Trail 1105A) and continue 0.8 mile to the junction with Trail 1104A. Turn right and walk 500 feet to see the largest of the ponds known collectively as Blankenship Lakes. Tumac Mountain (Hike 46) rises serenely

Low water levels in 2001 revealed the volcanic rock that makes up the beds of the Blankenship Lakes. (Photo by Alan L. Bauer)

over the 5245-foot lake, which is ringed by a number of excellent spots for a midday snack.

When rested, return to the junction, get back onto Trail 1105, and follow it for another 0.8 mile to the junction with Trail 979. Turn left onto 979 (Trail 1105 continues south to the area described in Hike 48) and walk north 0.9 mile past a small meadow to a junction with Pear Lake Trail 1148. Veer right onto 1148 and walk a short distance to the shore of Apple Lake, a picture-perfect pond of blue meltwater surrounded by a vast expanse of lush green meadow.

When the last of your film is exposed, continue on to more rugged

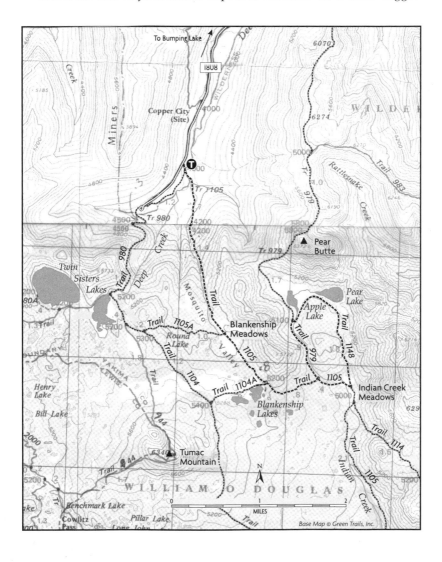

Pear Lake. The most accessible viewpoints are found immediately as the lake's western tip comes into view, for the official path stays a fair distance from the shore.

Trail 1148 leaves the lake, curls south through deep woods, and then steps onto the lush flats of Indian Creek Meadows, a picturesque oasis of grass and wildflowers. Pick up Trail 1105 amid the scenic greenery, wade (or leap) the babbling path of Indian Creek, then follow 1105 for 0.4 mile to find the path you hiked in from. From the junction, it is 3.7 familiar miles back to your vehicle.

48 INDIAN CREEK

Distance ■	9 miles (loop)
Hiking time ■	5 hours
Starting elevation ■	3393 feet
High point ■	4750 feet
Hikable ■	Mid-June through September
Maps ■	Green Trails 303 White Pass; USGS Spiral Butte
Information ■	Naches Ranger District, Wenatchee National Forest 509-653-2205 (ask about Trails 1105, 1109, 1104, 1147)

Late summer and early fall are probably the best times to hike this lower section of Indian Creek, as those who arrive too early might encounter clouds of mosquitoes and large swaths of hoof-churned muck. With some summer seasoning, this 9-mile loop lets hikers enjoy a pleasant afternoon of solitary strolling—save for a few horses and riders. Views are not spectacular, but the trail is mostly level and fairly accessible.

To reach the trailhead, turn north off US 12 onto Forest Service Road

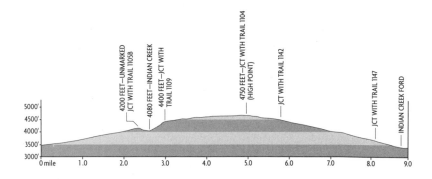

Hikers cross a footbridge at the bottom of a small canyon carved by Indian Creek. (Photo by Skip Card)

(FS) 1308. The turnoff is about 0.2 mile east of the Indian Creek Corrals, or about 300 feet west of the Indian Creek Campground. Follow FS 1308 for 2.6 miles until it dead-ends at a broad trailhead big enough for horse trailers. An outhouse is available, and on-site wilderness registration is required. (Drivers of low-riding passenger vehicles too fragile for gravel roads can use an alternative trailhead just off US 12, about a mile west of the Indian Creek Corrals. Starting the hike here adds 1.4 miles to the round trip, since hikers must walk 0.7 mile along Trail 1104 to connect with the loop.)

The southern end of Indian Creek Trail 1105 begins broadly but narrows about 0.5 mile from the trailhead when hikers enter the William O. Douglas Wilderness. The often dry and relatively rocky path runs parallel to Indian Creek as it passes through shading stands of western hemlock sprinkled with a few Douglas fir.

About 2.4 miles of gentle uphill walking bring hikers to 4200 feet, site of a clearing and an unmarked junction with broad Trail 1105B. Do not bother with it. The tree-strewn trail heads steeply uphill and tops out at 4842 feet after 1.1 miles, a good distance from any worthwhile views and far short of the crest of 6658-foot McNeil Peak.

Instead, descend steeply down to the footbridge at the bottom of a picturesque canyon with walls scoured by Indian Creek's occasional outbursts. As you switchback up the far side, from time to time meander off the trail through the brush to creekside overlooks. You might catch a

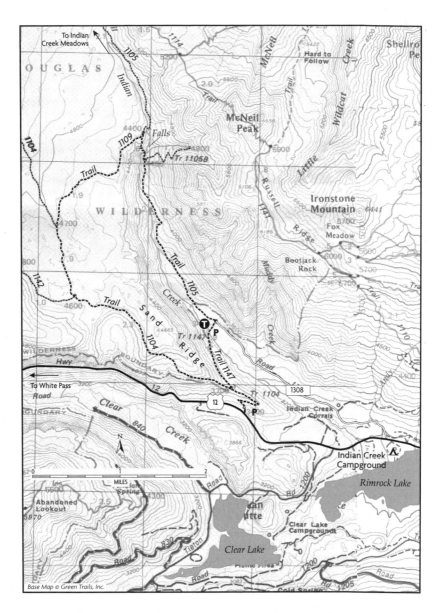

glimpse of Indian Creek Falls, a bit of scenery that the original trail builders chose not to include in the tour.

The trek up and out of the canyon tops out at the creekside junction
with Trail 1109. Trail 1105 continues north, toward Indian Creek Meadows
and Blankenship Lakes (Hike 47). Turn left here onto 1109 and begin a

stretch of mostly level terrain. The journey is fast and easy except for places where the trail bogs down into a marshy mess. Horses plow straight through; hikers typically scout a detour.

After 1.9 miles, veer left at a junction with Sand Ridge Trail 1104. Continue your mostly flat mush through the marshes for another 0.9 mile, and stay left at another junction to remain on Trail 1104. Some alpine scenery reveals itself a short distance beyond the junction where the trail skirts a rocky bowl that looks out toward 5970-foot Round Mountain.

The descent steepens as the trail heads down the nose of Sand Ridge. Turn left after 2.3 miles at the junction with Trail 1147 (unless you parked your vehicle at the trailhead just off the highway) and drop down 0.7 mile to Indian Creek. There is no footbridge, so wade the cold waters or tiptoe across a fallen log to reach the far shore. The parking lot looms a quick 0.2 mile distant.

49 ∶ KILLEN CREEK

Distance ■	8.2 miles (round trip)
Hiking time ■	6.5 hours
Starting point ■	4600 feet
High point ■	6900 feet
Hikable ■	August to early October
Maps ■	Green Trails 366 Mount Adams West and 334 Blue Lake, or 367S Mount Adams; USGS Mount Adams Wilderness
Information ■	Trout Lake Ranger District, Gifford Pinchot National Forest, 509-395-3402 (ask about Killen Creek Trail 113)

This trail takes hikers to a climbers' camp offering a closeup of Pa-toe, the native name given to 12,276-foot Mount Adams. Seattle residents tend to forget Mount Adams, since it is virtually invisible from Western Washington. Captain Vancouver did not even know the peak existed when he explored Puget Sound—Adams was too far east, and Mount St. Helens blocked it from view. The peak got its modern name in 1850, when a geographer trying to rename Mount Hood in honor of John Adams accidentally bestowed the presidential moniker on its taller northern

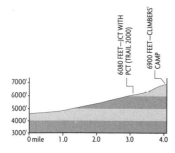

neighbor. The mistake was eventually discovered, but by then officials decided to leave Hood as is and let Adams remain Adams.

Adams' out-of-the-way location may rob the peak of publicity, but it offers other advantages. Precipitation moving east from the Pacific often gets blocked by Mount St. Helens and Mount Hood. But Adams still receives its fair share of snow each winter, and hikers who trek up Killen Creek to what are called the Upper Meadows will likely find snow at higher elevations well into early August, when wildflowers typically make their appearance. By September, the snow is usually gone, the weather dry, and a few flowers still in bloom.

From the town of Randle on US 12, turn south on the road pointing to Mount St. Helens National Volcanic Monument and Trout Lake. In just under a mile, turn left on Forest Service Road (FS) 23 and stay on this road for about 33 miles. The road is mostly paved but has an 11-mile stretch of dusty gravel that will rattle but not ruin passenger vehicles. After 33 miles, turn left on FS 2329 and circle around Takhlakh Lake—a great overnight camping spot for those not backpacking. The trailhead for Trail 113 is 6.3 miles from the turnoff; if you reach Killen Creek Campground, you have gone too far.

Trail 113 begins at 4600 feet and climbs steadily through heavy forest with limited views. After 2 miles, the trail breaks out of the forest and into a small meadow, a worthy resting spot for anyone with a full backpack.

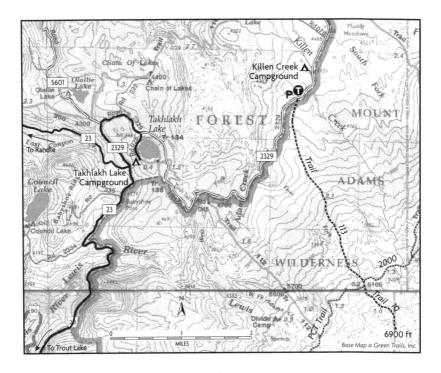

View of Mount Adams from high camp. (Photo by Dennis Long)

After 3.1 miles, hikers reach a 6080-foot junction with Trail 2000, better known as the Pacific Crest Trail. Cross over the trail and continue on an unmaintained trail, shown on some maps as Trail 10. Although not regularly cleared of downed trees and other hazards, Trail 10 is easy to follow given the hundreds (perhaps thousands) of hikers who take this journey every summer. After 1 mile and 800 feet of elevation gain, the trail ends in a meadow laced with creeks of melting snow and graced with grand views of Mount Rainier, Mount St. Helens, and, of course, Mount Adams.

This 6900-foot upper meadow is used as a base camp for climbers attempting Mount Adams' north ridge or one of its north-facing glaciers. All are technical climbs requiring specific equipment and expertise; hikers who lack either should go no higher. Hikers are welcome to camp here, but they should pitch tents in a spot that has been used previously and should retire quietly and early along with the climbers.

Those who must turn around should be sure to soak up the views before trudging down to their vehicles. Those with luck and foresight will have secured a campsite at Takhlakh Lake so they can enjoy another day in the area and do another hike.

50 ┊ INDIAN HEAVEN

Option 1
Distance ■ **15.1 miles (one way)**
Hiking time ■ 6 to 7 hours (day hike), 2 days (overnight trip)
Starting elevation ■ 3988 feet
High point ■ 5100 feet

Option 2
Distance ■ **9.7 miles (loop)**
Hiking time ■ 4 to 5 hours
Starting elevation ■ 3988 feet
High point ■ 5237 feet

Open and hikable ■ Mid-July to September
Maps ■ Green Trails 365 Lone Butte and 397 Wind River; USGS Lone Butte and Gifford Peak
Information ■ Mount Adams Ranger District, Gifford Pinchot National Forest, 360-395-3402 (ask about Indian Heaven Wilderness trails between Roads 24 and 60)

Options abound amid the looping paths of the Indian Heaven Wilderness, a small oasis of protected forest in the shadow of Mount Adams. More than a dozen alpine lakes dot the lowlands, providing scenic rest spots to dip a toe. Nearby, exposed ridge tops offer big views amid delicate wildflowers. Linking all this scenery are paths that meander (with manageable elevation gains) through shady forests interrupted by meadows of blue huckleberries. *Two cautions:* First, time your trip to sample the berries but avoid the clouds

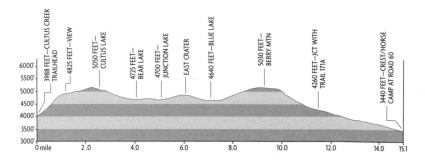

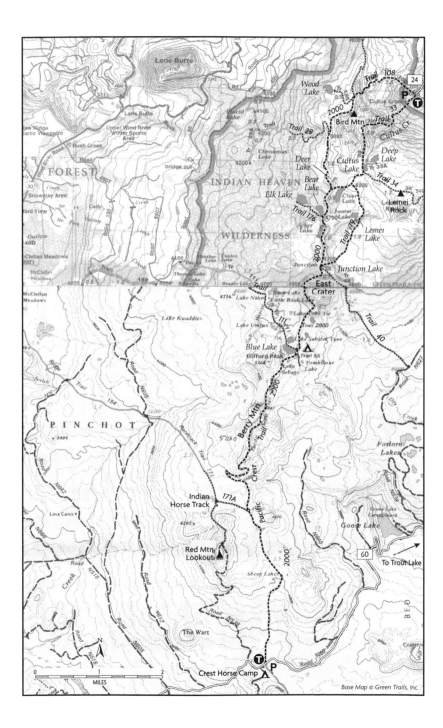

Blue Lake in the Indian Heaven Wilderness. (Photo by Skip Card)

of bloodthirsty mosquitoes that erupt each July when the snowmelt turns meadows to marshes. Second, carry a map and compass; some signposts at key junctions are missing or hard to spot.

To reach the northern trailhead, head west out of Trout Lake on State Route 141 (which becomes Forest Service Road 60) and drive 7.2 miles beyond the ranger station to the Peterson Prairie Campground. Turn right onto

Forest Service Road (FS) 24 and follow the washboard gravel for 9 miles to Cultus Creek Campground. Turn left into the campground and loop around to the trailhead parking lot, following signs to Indian Heaven Trail 33. The trailhead for Trail 108 (a steeper path best saved for the descent of the loop hike) joins FS 24 just beyond the Cultus Creek Campground.

Through-hikers or backpackers who want to leave a vehicle at the southern trailhead should drive to the Peterson Prairie Campground and continue on FS 60 another 10 miles to the Crest Horse Camp. The tiny camp is on the left side of the road about 4.5 miles beyond the Goose Lake Campground. On-site registration is required at both trailheads.

All Indian Heaven trips are best begun on Trail 33, which climbs steadily up a hillside shaded by hemlock and pine. Views are few until the path steps onto an exposed ridge 1 mile from the trailhead. At 4825 feet, a switchback reveals Mount Adams, Mount Rainier, the Goat Rocks, and a panorama of forested foothills. The trail climbs more gradually another 1.5 miles until hikers reach 5050-foot Cultus Lake, the first of the area's many snow-fed pools.

Route options begin 0.5 mile beyond the lake. Hikers who want to loop back to their vehicles should veer left at a junction with Trail 179 and walk 1.9 miles of gently descending trail to Junction Lake and a connection with Trail 2000, better known as the Pacific Crest Trail (PCT). After a restful break, head north on the PCT past Bear Lake and toward Bird Mountain. After 3.5 miles, veer east onto Trail 108 and soon top out at a 5237-foot gap offering excellent alpine views. A steep descent returns hikers to FS 24, just a short walk from their vehicles at the campground trailhead.

Hikers or backpackers who have arranged transportation should likewise head south from Cultus Lake but then veer right at the junction with Trail 179, staying on the sometimes faint Trail 33 through boggy meadows toward a connection with the PCT. Turn south onto the PCT toward Bear Lake, go a mile to Junction Lake, then follow the PCT another 2.2 miles as it skirts below East Crater (not much crater, too many trees) and descends to Blue Lake. Campsites near the lake provide worthy overnight stopovers so long as bugs are not bad.

Beyond Blue Lake, the PCT rises slowly but steadily to the crest of Berry Mountain, a long ridge offering views of Mount St. Helens' southeastern flank. Wildflowers are often abundant on the narrow mountain's sunbaked crest, which tops out at about 5030 feet.

It is all downhill from here. The trail switchbacks in broad sweeps down the southern nose of Berry Mountain, passing through thin trees that reveal 4968-foot Red Mountain and its crowning fire lookout. After an initially steep descent, the terrain flattens somewhat but continues downhill to a junction with Trail 171A, a connector path leading to the faint outlines of an old Indian horse track. Another 3.5 miles of gentle descent take hikers to FS 60, where they can congratulate themselves for covering 15.1 miles in a single day.

REFERENCES

Laskin, David. *Rains All the Time: A Connoisseur's History of Weather in the Pacific Northwest.* Seattle: Sasquatch Books, 1997.

May, Allan. *Longstreet Highroad Guide to the Washington Cascades.* Atlanta: Longstreet, 1999.

Renner, Jeff. *Northwest Mountain Weather: Understanding and Forecasting for the Backcountry User.* Seattle: The Mountaineers Books, 1992.

Spring, Ira, and Harvey Manning. *50 Hikes in Mount Rainier National Park,* 4th edition. Seattle: The Mountaineers Books, 1999.

———. *100 Hikes in the South Cascades and Olympics,* 3rd edition. Seattle: The Mountaineers Books, 1998.

———. *100 Hikes in Washington's North Cascades National Park Region,* 3rd edition. Seattle: The Mountaineers Books, 2000.

Spring, Ira, Vicky Spring, and Harvey Manning. *100 Hikes in Washington's Alpine Lakes,* 3rd edition. Seattle: The Mountaineers Books, 2000.

U.S. Geological Survey and U.S. Bureau of Mines. *Mineral Resources of the Alpine Lake Study Area.* Washington, D.C.: U.S. Government Printing Office, 1989.

Walker, Wendy. *Washington National Forests.* Helena, Montana: Falcon Press, 1992.

SUGGESTED READING

Aanthes, Richard. *Meteorology*. Upper Saddle River, New Jersey: Prentice Hall, 1997.

Chaston, Peter. *Weather Maps: How to Read and Interpret All the Basic Weather Charts*. Kearney, Missouri: Chaston Scientific, 1995.

Keen, Richard. *Skywatch: The Western Weather Guide*. Golden, Colorado: Fulcrum, 1987.

Lilly, Kenneth. *Marine Weather of Western Washington*. Seattle: Starpath, 1983.

Renner, Jeff. *Lightning Strikes: Staying Safe Under Stormy Skies*. Seattle: The Mountaineers Books, 2002.

———. *Northwest Mountain Weather: Understanding and Forecasting for the Backcountry User*. Seattle: The Mountaineers Books, 1992.

Stull, Roland. *Meteorology for Scientists and Engineers*. Pacific Grove, California: Brooks/Cole, 2000.

Whiteman, C. David. *Mountain Meteorology*. New York: Oxford University Press, 2000.

INDEX

Numbers in *italics* indicate photographs and illustrations

adiabatic lapse rate, 11
Aleutian Low, 13
Alpine Lookout, 80–84
altimeter as forecasting tool, 21–22
altocumulus clouds, *19, 20,* 20–21
altostratus clouds, 24, *25*
American Ridge, 181–183
barometric pressure, 13
Basalt Pass, 77–80
Basalt Peak, 79
Bean Creek Basin, 122–124
Berry Mountain, 199
Blankenship Lakes, 187–190
Blewett Pass, 8
blocking high, 15
Buckhorn Mountain, 52–54
Burroughs Mountain, 154–157
Burrows Channel, 42
campfires, 33, 76
Canyon Creek, 63–65
Cathedral Pass, 108–109
Cathedral Rock, 108–109
Chinook Pass, 172
Chiwaukum Lake, 86, 90
cirrus clouds, 21–22, *21, 22*
Colchuck Lake, 93–95
cold fronts, 15
continental climate, 8–10
contrails, 22, *23*
Corral Pass, 148, 165
Crystal Peak, 167–170
cumulonimbus clouds, *20,* 21
Dalles Ridge, 163
Davis Peak, 109–112
Deer Park, 46–48
Diamond Lake, 102–103
divine forecasting, 21–26
Dungeness National Wildlife
    Refuge, 43
Dungeness Spit, 36, 43–46

Ebey, Isaac, 58
Ebey's Landing, 57–60
Eightmile Lake, 92
El Niño, 16
Elk Mountain, 47–49
Enchantments, 95
Falls Creek, 129
Ferguson Lake, 69–71
Fidalgo Head loop, 40–43
Fifes Ridge, 175–178
Fishhook Flats, 143–144
Forks, 13, 36
Fort Ebey State Park, 60
Fort Casey State Park, 60
French Cabin Mountain, 104–106
Goat Peak, 182–183
Gold Ridge Tarn, 66–68
Grand Park, 151–154
Harding Mountain, 98
Hart, Col. W. Thomas, 69
Harts Pass, 62, 66, 69
Hidden Lake, 157–159
Indian Creek, 190–193
Indian Creek Meadows, 190
Ingalls Creek, 14, 127–130
Ingalls Pass, 119
Iron Creek, 133
Iron Peak, 124–127
Iron Mountain, 54
Jack Creek, 96–98
jet stream, 15–16
Kachess Beacon Tower, 104
Kachess Ridge, 103–105
Kelly Butte, 149–151
Killen Creek, 193–195
La Niña, 16
Lake Ann, 115–118
Lake Caroline, 90, 92
Lake Donald, 84–87
Lake Ingalls, 118–121

Lake Julius, 84–87
Larch Lake, 87–90
Leavenworth, 12, 76
lenticular clouds, 22–24, 24
lightning, 19–21
Loch Eileen, 84–87
Longs Pass, 119
marine climate, 8–10
marine push, 18–19
Marmot Pass, 54
Meadow Creek, 98
Miller Peak, 131–133
Moran, Robert, 39
Moran State Park, 37, 39
Mosquito Valley, 187–188
Mount Adams, 193–195
Mount Aix, 178–181
Mount Baker, 62
Mount Constitution, 37–40
Mount Daniel, 100
Mount Olympus, 8
Mount Ellinor, 55–57
Mount Rainier, 148, 168–169
Mount Rainier National Park, 32,
    148–162, 167–170
Mount Rolo, 71
Mount Townsend, 49–52
Mount Washington, 56
Nason Ridge, 83
Navaho Pass, 139–142
Navaho Peak, 142
New Dungeness Lighthouse, 45–46
nimbostratus clouds, 24, 26
Noble Knob, 162–165
Norse Peak, 165–167
North Cascades National Park, 31
Northwest Forest Pass, 31–32
Obstruction Point, 46–49
Olympic National Park, 32
Orcas Island, 37
Osceola Mudflow, 156–157, 169
Pacific High, 13
Palisades Lakes Trail, 157–161
Peggy's Pond, 106–109
Perego's Lake, 58

pets, 33
Polallie Ridge, 101–103
Pugh Ridge, 62, 72–74
Puget Sound Convergence Zone,
    17–18, 17, 24
Pyramid Mountain, 74
rain shadow effect, 11, 12
Rainier, Peter, 148
Robert Pratt Preserve, 58
Rowley, Jack, 65
safety, 34
Salmon la Sac, 100
Scottish Lakes High Camp, 87, 90
Sequim, 8, 36
Silver Lake, 68
Slide Mountain, 159–162
Snoqualmie Pass, 8
Sourdough Gap, 173–175
Sourdough Mountains, 160–162
Standup Creek Trail, 142
Standup Pass, 142
Stevens Pass, 12, 76
storm track, 13
stratus clouds, 24, 25
Stuart Pass, 129
summer monsoonal flow, 19
Taneum Creek, 143–144
Taneum Ridge, 142–146
Teanaway Ridge, 133–135
Teanaway River Valley, 114
Ten Essentials, 27
Three Brothers, 129
Tronsen Ridge, 135–139
Twin Sisters Lakes, 184
Tumac Mountain, 184–187
Van Epps Pass, 118
warm fronts, 15
Washington Park, 41
Washington state ferries, 37
waste disposal, 33
Whidbey Island, 57
wilderness ethics, 32–33
wildfires, 76
William O. Douglas Wilderness, 181
Windy Pass, 90–93

ACKNOWLEDGMENTS

The seeds for this book were sown in 1976, when Michael Fagin made his first backpacking trip to Washington's Olympic rain forest—a trip he describes as very enlightening and very wet. During this soggy journey, Michael discovered the value and joy of finding dry hikes, and his passion led him to discover and chart Washington's rain shadow regions. In spring and fall, Michael quickly set a routine: He would forecast on Friday, hike the ridges and peaks over the weekend to confirm the forecast, and then record what he had learned.

Michael would never have made this journey without the help of some friends. First and foremost is Dennis Long, who shared his thirty years of Northwest hiking experience and his passion for the mountains. Writer Denis DuBois worked with Michael to create the format for this book, an important step. Another key contributor is Alan Bauer, whose unique photography provides an essential ingredient that displays the beauty of these hikes in the best possible light.

Special thanks go to Dr. Nick Bond, research meteorologist at the University of Washington, for reviewing the weather introduction. Thanks, too, to geology instructor Ralph Hitz of Tacoma Community College for his help in identifying rock formations.

Skip Card thanks longtime hiking buddies Eric and Traci Degerman and Sandi Doughton, three wonderful friends who kept him company on otherwise lonely trails. Skip also thanks Executive Editor David Zeeck and the other senior editors at *The News Tribune* for allowing him to work on this book. *News Tribune* graphic artist Fred Matamoros earns praise for his illustrations (delivered on deadline, as usual) in the weather section.

Both authors thank project editor Christine "Cat Woman" Hosler of The Mountaineers Books for her guidance, and copyeditor Heath Lynn Silberfeld for her sharp-eyed attention to detail.

Michael thanks Skip for taking his mangled writing style and making it flow like a pro's. Skip thanks Michael for welcoming him onto this project, sight unseen, long after all the work of sifting rainfall data and selecting trails had been completed.

ABOUT THE AUTHORS

MICHAEL FAGIN is the lead forecaster for Washington Online Weather, a website *(www.wowweather.com)* and custom forecast service that has provided mountain weather forecasts since 1996. He has been active in mountaineering since 1976 and has hiked, scrambled, snowshoed, or skied all the major regions of Washington state; he has shared his weekly hiking tips on Northwest Cable News. He is involved with other private forecasting companies and gives mountain weather lectures around the region.

SKIP CARD, a professional journalist since graduating from the University of Washington in 1986, writes about outdoor recreation and national parks for *The News Tribune* of Tacoma. He is a lifelong Washington resident and has long been active in a variety of outdoor activities, particularly hiking, climbing, and skiing. His articles about Mount Rainier have won several awards from the Society of Professional Journalists.

Michael Fagin   *Skip Card*

THE MOUNTAINEERS, founded in 1906, is a nonprofit outdoor activity and conservation club with 15,000 members, whose mission is "to explore, study, preserve, and enjoy the natural beauty of the outdoors. . . ." The club sponsors many classes and year-round outdoor activities in the Pacific Northwest,and supports environmental causes through educational activities, sponsoring legislation and presenting educational programs. The Mountaineers Books supports the club's mission by publishing travel and natural history guides, instructional texts, and works on conservation and history.

Send or call for our catalog of more than 500 outdoor titles:

The Mountaineers Books
1001 SW Klickitat Way, Suite 201
Seattle, WA 98134
800-553-4453
mbooks@mountaineers.org
www.mountaineersbooks.org

The Mountaineers Books is proud to be a corporate sponsor of Leave No Trace, whose mission is to promote and inspire responsible outdoor recreation through education, research, and partnerships. The Leave No Trace program is focused specifically on human-powered (nonmotorized) recreation.

Leave No Trace strives to educate visitors about the nature of their recreational impacts, as well as offer techniques to prevent and minimize such impacts. Leave No Trace is best understood as an educational and ethical program, not as a set of rules and regulations.

For more information, visit *www.lnt.org*, or call 800-332-4100.

Green Trails, Inc., founded in 1973, publishes more than 125 topographic recreation map titles for the mountain and beach areas of Washington and Oregon's Cascade Mountains and Washington's Olympic Peninsula. Green Trails maps show current trail, road, and access information to national forests, national parks, state and local parks, and other public lands in the most clear, compact, and convenient format and scale available.

Green Trails maps have been the Northwest's first choice for hiking, backpacking, walking, climbing, mountaineering, cross-country skiing, mountain biking, fishing, horseback riding, and hunting for 30 years.

For more information, visit *www.greentrailsmaps.com* or call (206) 546-6277.

OTHER TITLES YOU MIGHT ENJOY FROM THE MOUNTAINEERS BOOKS

Available at fine bookstores and outdoor stores, by phone at
(800) 553-4453, or on the Web at *www.mountaineersbooks.org*

Best Loop Hikes in Washington by Dan Nelson, photography by Alan Bauer.
$16.95 paperbound. 0-89886-866-1.

Hidden Hikes in Western Washington by Karen Sykes. $16.95 paperbound.
0-89886-859-9.

Roads to Trails: Northwest Washington by Washington Trails Association
Volunteers, coordinated by Ira Spring. $14.95 paperbound.
0-89886-875-0.

*Exploring Washington's Wild Areas: A Guide for Hikers, Backpackers,
Climbers, Cross-Country Skiers, and Paddlers, 2nd Edition*
by Marge and Ted Mueller. $18.95 paperbound. 0-89886-807-6.

100 Classic Hikes in™ Washington by Ira Spring and Harvey Manning.
$19.95 paperbound. 0-89886-586-7.

Best of the Pacific Crest Trail: Washington: 55 Hikes by Dan Nelson. $16.95
paperback. 0-89886-703-7.

Hiking Washington's Geology by Scott Babcock and Robert Carson. $16.95
paperbound. 0-89886-548-4.

Animal Tracks of the Pacific Northwest by Karen Pandell and Chris Stall.
$6.95 paperbound. 0-89886-012-1.

Mountain Flowers of the Cascades and Olympics, 2nd Edition
by Harvey Manning, photographs by Bob and Ira Spring. $9.95
spiral bound. 0-89886-883-1.

Northwest Trees by Stephen F. Arno and Ramona P. Hammerly. $14.95
paperbound. 0-916890-50-3.

*Northwest Mountain Weather: Understanding and Forecasting for the
Backcountry User* by Jeff Renner. $10.95 paperbound. 0-89886-297-3.